A FOUNTAIN OF TRUTH

A
FOUNTAIN OF TRUTH

A Collection of Sunday Lectures
by
various ministers of
Religious Science

Presented by
Merle A. Kehoe

First Edition

DeVorss & Company, Publisher
1046 Princeton Drive
Marina del Rey, California 90291

Printed in the United States of America
by Book Graphics, Inc., California

cover design: gary
peattie

Recognition

. . . that all inspiration and creativity springs forth from the Source, God.

Contents

Introduction

This book came into being as the result of a thought which was floating around in the universe. When it first made itself known, the idea was more or less put aside in a very human way with words such as, "Can't happen—too many unknowns," and so on.

However, the idea would not permit itself to be laid to rest. It kept returning, and it seemed as though it were saying, "If I don't come into being, there had better be a pretty good reason why not."

The first steps were finally taken. From then on, everything went forward perfectly.

This book has eighteen "authors," in that it is composed of eighteen Sunday lectures, or lessons, delivered by eighteen ministers of Religious Science to their listeners. Two of the talks were broadcast by radio.

When the ministers who are represented in this volume were delivering their lectures, they had no inkling that those talks eventually would be edited and become chapters of a book.

Every effort has been made by the editors—and by the ministers themselves who reviewed and sometimes helped in editing their own lectures—to present the talks in a casual but interesting literary form. The editors also strove to preserve the unique style of each speaker.

Another aim was to present the lessons in such a way that the reader might almost feel that he or she was actually present when they were given. We believe that much of what was desired has been achieved and that the overall approach used will be pleasantly effective to the mind of the reader.

Each lesson is arranged according to the alphabetical listing of the name of the minister who gave it. Since there are no subject categories and because each chapter is complete in itself, the reader should begin where led to begin. There is no "outcome" in the final chapter, and the rest of the book will not be affected for the reader if he or she should choose to read the last chapter first.

This collection is not intended to be the "be all and end all" of what Religious Science has to say. The volume is a purely private undertaking and contains only the free expressions of the contributing ministers. No religious organization is connected with the publication of this volume in any way.

Now, as to the talks themselves, are they good? Are the ideas presented helpful? Are the talks inspirational, instructive, and informative?

We will let the talks speak for themselves.

—the editors

CHAPTER ONE

To accuse others for one's own misfortunes is a sign of want of education. To accuse one's self shows that one's education has begun. But to accuse neither one's self nor others shows that one's education is complete.

—Epictetus

You Don't Need Problems to Have Rewards

Reverend Nancy Anderson

Thursday night in class I asked the people there if the word "divine" meant anything to them—we are always saying, "Divine Mind," divine this, divine that—and I got a lot of blanks. And then I said, "Let's think about it. What does Divine Mind mean to you?" And some ideas started coming forth; basically the idea of "knowingness." Divine, "I know, I understand." Let's think about that.

We're saying that there is a Divine Mind, an All-Knowing Mind, that not only knows everything but knows how to produce an effect of Itself in any way that It chooses at any time, that It is the only Power, that It is the only Presence, and that It is everywhere. And that Mind is my mind, and that Mind is your mind.

How much do we know that of ourselves? I believe that to the degree that we know it is the degree of ease of a flowing good in our life. To the degree that we don't know it—and because we don't know it—we're seeking to have

1

the results of what that means to us, but without knowing that it is that lack of knowledge which causes us to have what we call problems, the painful experiences of life that we don't want. I feel that we have to raise our own level of understanding considerably. I feel that too many of us believe that our answers in life—that is, the things we like in life—have to come to us as a result of suffering.

There is a delightful book that is going to be published one of these days that was written by one of our members. I can give it a plug in advance. In there he has a cartoon of a little boy who was talking to this little girl, and he's saying, "What's happiness?" She answers, "Happiness is relative, Alfie. One must suffer first to truly achieve it." So he got this look on his face and he said, "Oh, I'm in phase one of happiness!" I think sometimes that's what we believe— "in order to have the happiness, I've got to go through that phase one part." If we have that opinion I'd like to change it.

Until we reach, I believe, the point of seeing that the answers we want exist on other than the physical plane of life and that there are really answers in self-awareness, we are going to be going through a process. This process will be of mentally forming a concept of what we think is our answer, doing our work in mind until we achieve that effect, and then finding that we have not really achieved what we wanted; then we will go back and try to re-think it and say, "What did I do wrong? Why wasn't that my right answer?" And we can go on and on, as though we were on a treadmill, and become very discouraged.

What we really want are the rewards of living. The title of my talk today is suggesting to you that you don't have to have the problems in order to have the rewards. I have found, in my moments of self-honesty, that I have used problems in order to get rewards.

Hasn't it felt good to make up with somebody you had a

quarrel with? Doesn't it feel good to come back into that nice sense of unity and oneness? Have you felt it was almost good enough to have gone through the experience of the argument because it felt so good afterwards? Haven't you at times actually put yourself through a problem where you felt needy and down and depressed—and then somebody came along and picked you up emotionally and gave you some encouraging ideas and you felt so loved? I have put myself through that, and I've also come to realize that I was putting myself through that because I wanted the experience of what I called being loved. And I've gotten a little tired of it.

Have you had people in your life that have been on the other side of this, where you felt so good about yourself and about your importance because you were needed, that you were really making a demand upon life to keep you in a position with others needing you? Did you find that that was just fine, until they got to be a burden? Did you feel they were depending on you too much? Did you feel your strength and vitality being sapped? Did you wonder why you were doing it?

Let's remember that we must take responsibility and that our consciousness automatically creates the effect that will best fulfill. This fulfillment happens because there is an Intelligence at work.

If we want to feel a sense of achievement and a sense of value, sometimes I believe we think, "If I overcome obstacles and really struggle through, and then achieve, I'm going to get added recognition and I'm going to feel a little bit more worthwhile." If I think that, my mind creates problems for me to struggle through, and then I can say, "Look, I really hung in there, it really worked!" And I would feel pleased, of course, with the result, but also pleased with having gone through that process.

Truly, you know, our programmed ignorance, shall I say, is going to cause enough obstacles. We don't need to add any others.

Let's recognize that what we were looking for in all those circumstances was an experience of love, an experience of inner value, and an experience, perhaps, of security. And truly we were creating pseudo-answers, and we were making ourselves repeat circumstances to get those rewards.

There is no tangible experience that will make a person feel secure if he is inwardly insecure. There is no experience of so-called love that will give you the feeling, permanently, of being loved unless you know that you are love itself, and that you are valuable, and that you appreciate yourself and that you appreciate that same self in the other people of your world.

I am going to quote from a writing of a man I admire, Tom Johnson: "Whatever we are actively seeking always flies away from us, because it is the law of life that we only have what we give or express."

Happiness in all forms is that which flows out from us rather than to us. When you are aware of the reality of consciousness, and that within consciousness is all that we will ever need or can ever have, the goal becomes the understanding of the true self rather than the pursuit of things.

Ask yourself about your life. What are you doing? Is it a joy? Are you having fun with it? Do you feel free and flowing and expansive and at ease? Are you happy? You see, that's what you want. You want to be happy with yourself and with what your life is. If you're in the midst of a so-called problem right now, insist that your mind see it in terms of the ideas that you are holding about yourself or about life. If you are experiencing conflict and you're having static from people, see where your inner conflict is producing that and returning it to you. Basically what we put out reverberates like an echo from a canyon wall. Another example which is very common is that these ideas are mirrored or reflected to us. So, you know, accept that. It's your key to freedom. It's your way out of your difficulty, because it means that a new idea can be born within your consciousness. Remember, your mind is an aspect, a point of awareness, in a total creative mind that has all answers already in it because it *is* the answer.

You don't go to God to get an answer. You go to God, to the Truth within you, to become aware of that Truth— and that is the answer. That's the answer because there is no problem. Within God there is no problem; there's just a continuing flow of Itself. And I think too many times we go through life as the person who feels so good after it stops hurting that he wants to go through the hurt once more so that it feels so good again.

Ask yourself, "Do I have to hear a discordant note on a piano in order to appreciate good music?" I don't. I can just appreciate it. I don't have to have the contrast any more. I'm believing that. I'm establishing that.

When you become aware of what you want in life, start to think and talk and act in its terms. I don't mean you should tell the world your goals. I think your personal goals should be private to you except as they are shared with those who are in harmony and who are working with you towards them. But start to think and act and talk in its terms. Sometimes we have a goal, but because that goal is not yet reached, we see the effect which seems to indicate the goal is not reached; and then we fuss and worry and talk in terms of what we don't want. And, of course, the law of mind takes the idea presented to it and automatically produces what we don't want.

Recognize that we can change our thinking. What we really want to experience is our real self. When we believe the good is outside of us, we are seeking to get it. And that attitude of seeking to get a good is the problem. It's a belief that we are less than the good itself, that we are not the cause of the supply of everything we want in our life; it's the attitude that creates the experience we call limitation, lack, conflict, loneliness, all of the things we do not want to experience. Our belief that we are not okay, that something is missing within us, causes us to feel insecure; and that idea of insecurity keeps producing experiences that verify our belief that we are not okay.

One of the things that I have come to recognize is that nothing is going to happen out there in my world of experience that I would be afraid of unless I keep the fear. When I was a child I can remember being told many times the statement of Franklin Roosevelt that we have nothing to fear but fear itself. I don't know whether it was original with him, but he said a good line there.

The belief that I am without that which I need or what I have that is important to me will be taken away is a *belief*. The belief produces the experience I don't want. But if I don't believe it, it's not going to happen. So we're being afraid of shadows, aren't we? We're being afraid of something that doesn't exist. You're going to alleviate your problem by getting at the root of it, the root idea. I might believe that I have run out of Truth. Right? If I believe I have run out of Truth, that I have run out of that which I need, I am, of course, afraid. But that is not so. I am part of my supply in the sense that I am the channel through which supply takes place in my world. I am that because of what I am. To stop condemning ourselves is absolutely the first essential.

The philosopher Epictetus said, "To accuse others for one's own misfortunes is a sign of want of education. To accuse one's self shows that one's education has begun.

But to accuse neither one's self nor others shows that one's education is complete.'' I like that because I feel it's important that our idea of accepting responsibility or accountability for what's in our consciousness now is not an act of self-accusation. We have all been inundated with the ideas that are not correct about the reality of who we are. Those ideas have had their effect in our life. But you and I are spiritually mature people. We don't have to grow in order to be what we are. We may be individually growing in our awareness of it, but we are a complete being and it will reveal to us the idea that we need for that expression right now. And we don't have to become anything, but we have to recognize what we already are. How are you going to accept good if you don't believe you're worth it? In terms of life there's no question of this. It isn't an issue. You *are* it. You *are* your good.

Let us think: "I am my own good. I am the ongoing, continuous expression of all that is life, of all that is good. And this is mine to realize and then to express into my world.''

When are you happy? I know when I'm happy. It's when I'm feeling expansive, when I'm being myself, when I am giving, when I feel free to give a dollar or a flower, when I feel that I can say to someone, "I really love you, I enjoy you, I appreciate you." When I'm in that attitude of experiencing myself through expressing, I feel good. I enjoy it when someone does those things towards me. But I've found that if they are not, it is because I'm blocked off on the giving side. And it could be that I have blocked myself off and have had a sense of self-depreciation which I may not even be aware of at times.

Let's rise in our consciousness to our own true level, because we want to live normally. Spiritual living is normal living. We have so many newspaper articles about all of the other things that are going on, things that are abnormal, and they get people's attention. It seems as though we don't have our attention gained by that which is the normal. If you will train your mind to be appreciative of yourself, of what you are, and to really be aware of that, and to really be aware of this magnificent self in others and of this marvelous universe in which we live, that attitude is going to make you more and more aware of it and more and more expressive of it, and you're going to live in a state of continuing joy. That's what you want.

If philosophy isn't common sense it isn't good philosophy. And if religion isn't common sense it isn't good religion. I believe that our religion is absolutely marvelous common sense. I mean it's recognizable to any of us if we will pay attention to it. What we're saying, basically, is that "my image of myself creates my world and I have to have an accurate image of myself." That image is only going to be gained through an inner perception. It can never be gained by comparison of me with this person or that person or where I was or where I think I ought to be.

If you have that inner sense of self-appreciation, you don't have to do very much to have your world change. That attitude is going to bring into your life the people who will also appreciate you. It's going to open you to ideas of doing things you like; those ideas are going to be valuable to other people; and you are going to have the cooperation of other people. It's just the simple idea of "appreciating my very own self because I recognize the worth and value of being me."

Let's turn ourselves on to the idea that the sense of inner well-being which we call happiness will become basically what we experience all of the time.

If you are absorbed in sharing your happiness, living the ideas about yourself that you believe are true, being kind, being loving, giving—and the praying, which is your private time of personal self-awareness—not in order to let the truth be used by you but to let the truth use you to express itself in ways that will glorify your personal world and the world in which we live, our world has got to be transformed. So let's start with the basics, the understanding that the rewards of life are ours to accept—not to get— and then to share. I'm going to just know for you, for me, that each one of us has the capacity to do this and is doing it.

Albert Schweitzer said that we are not to despair of ourselves, that we are commanded to put our trust in God, not just in ourselves.

And as soon as I know myself as the ongoing expression of that God, my trust in God becomes my trust in my personal being, my personal ability to be aware of truth. That's my confidence, that's my security. And when I feel secure and confident, and I'm loving myself, the world automatically becomes a loving, happy, fulfilled place for me. And I'm going to know that we're doing that, all of us, right now.

Reverend Nancy Anderson is pastor of the Church of Religious Science at Cardiff-by-the-Sea, California.

She became interested in Religious Science in 1963. Shortly after obtaining her Practitioner's License in 1969, she began a study group in her home. Ministerial studies were completed by her in 1974, and shortly thereafter, she started to establish her church, subsequently being ordained in 1978.

A few years ago, for a period of 6 months, Reverend Anderson had a daily fifteen-minute radio program, plus a weekly one-hour call-in radio show. Currently, she has a weekly half-hour radio program called "Uplift."

In addition to the work she devotes to the ministry and to her radio show she finds time to be a frequent contributor to Creative Thought Magazine.

The talk, "You Don't Need Problems to Have Rewards," was given by Reverend Anderson at the Cardiff-by-the-Sea church on March 11, 1979.

CHAPTER TWO

We give up a great deal to other people. They don't take it from us. They invite it with a very strong personality and their need to dominate. But we have to give it up. If we do, that has been our decision, and we can always get it right back. You see, there's always a way out.

—Bair

The Spirit of Aloha

Reverend David Bair

Aloha kakahi aka. Which means good morning and welcome.

That was quite a nice ovation. Frankly, I don't think I would get that in my church, now that I think about it. Well, I do, but my church is not quite this large.

And I am going to take a moment right now to recognize just where I am, because it's quite an experience to stand up here for the first time, especially in this particular church which has a great deal of meaning for me. And it's fun to be in a real live church, with walls and ceilings, and a PA system that works, and lots of people out there.

I should share with you a little bit about how I got here in this church and got there in my church and what puts all of this together, because it's a very exciting success story in my life. And let's face it, we all enjoy the idea of success

11

even though we already are all successful. It's nice to know that you can do some things you want to do and to see the fulfillment.

It was just a short year ago that I was finishing my training, having no idea consciously of where I wanted to go. I finally decided that I was programming this experience, if you will, or setting myself up for this experience, perhaps as much as twenty-three years ago when I used to come to this church when it was the little chapel next door. I was in college here, and a very dear friend of mine who was my roommate at Los Angeles City College at the time, and I, came to hear lectures on Wednesday nights. Dr. Bitzer was here then, and that's when I first got to know him.

But there was another speaker who came here on Wednesday nights on occasion, and his name is Don Blanding. I'm sure you remember him. A very warm, loving, human being. He used to tell about his beautiful experiences in the islands. And so I'm going to allow him the credit for having planted that very wonderful seed in my mind many years ago, twenty-three, I believe, to not only go into ministry— or at least become involved in this teaching—but also to find a place like Hawaii to do it. And it's interesting that just a year later I found myself in the islands working on a film which was the last one of my youthful career in the picture business, but it was a very good start into public life, I think. And now all this time has passed, and something wonderful has happened.

As we look at the reasons, if we say that, or at the cause, we know what that's all about. We know that that seed was the cause and that I allowed it to manifest in my life over a relatively long period of time—which means that I was ready for it a year ago, perhaps not twenty years ago. But the idea was there. And, as we well know, everything starts with that idea—that's the beginning.

Everything that you and I experience, everything that

we are dealing with in our lives right now, begins in our minds as an idea. And I am very grateful and very full of joy today, as I reflect on this process and what has come about. And it has been very meaningful for me. I had to do much learning in life before I could teach effectively to others. And I have learned, and I am still learning, and I love what I am doing. And I'm in a wonderful place, and I'll share just a few things about it for those who may not have been to Kona.

Surprisingly enough, we are the only Religious Science Church in the islands and in the State of Hawaii. Very unusual. I'm not going to try to explain that one. There is a wonderful Unity church on the Island of Oahu, which I am having the pleasure of speaking at next month, in June. And it's great to see metaphysics and New Thought finally coming into its own in Hawaii after the fantastic history of the islands.

Our church is on the Big Island of Hawaii, the "Orchid Island," the "Volcano Island." We are on the Kona Coast, which, for years was a sleepy little fishing village. It ain't that way no more! We're seeing the growth there too; in fact, sometimes I think a little too much growth. We've already got too many cars and not enough roads to handle them. And you think you've got gasoline problems. I'm not sure whether there will be any gasoline when I get back because it does have to be shipped in, you know, like everything does.

But there is something wonderful about that island, the Big Island. If you've been there you know what I mean. The consciousness is high. The energy level is very high, and one of the reasons for that is that it's new land.

The history of the evolution of the Hawaiian Islands is immense in time and in scope. When you look at the northern island, you see land that has been there for millions of years. In fact, you don't even recognize its origin from lava flows. But you go down to the Big Island, and on the southern tip, just about thirty miles from where we are, here's land that's maybe twenty years old. Brand new land. And they're telling us that we might get some new land again soon. Fortunately, I believe it goes in the other direction. I haven't found that out yet. I look forward to telling you about that in the future—in person.

It is quite an exciting thing, though, to be a part of that kind of creation, that kind of energy. And I believe that there is some beautiful correlation between that energy and the consciousness of the people there. The Big Island has a tremendous amount of cultural tradition because of all the royalty that was born and fought and died there. And so it's very sacred ground.

I am thrilled with the attraction to have gone into my ministry right there. And now that I've been there a while, I'm recognizing the importance, the necessity, in my life, of learning more about metaphysics through Polynesia, which, as far as we know, could very well have been the beginning of, or at least closely associated with, mind science. And we are talking about thousands of years ago— long before most of the teachings that we are familiar with. Here was a people who were applying mental science in their life.

Of course, through the passage of time, much came along to change that. Perhaps that's why we are having a little challenge, shall we call it?—a good one—in reeducating the people in that area about New Thought, about Religious Science, about Science of Mind. You see, they had it natur- ally—many years ago. And then people came there and told them that most of it was all wrong. They changed their ways. And so there is much confusion. There are some who still cling to the old, but it is their way. There are others who have made the transformation into, let's say, the

Western Theology. And that has taken its toll. Now I see it all coming back together.

Just a couple of weeks ago all of the New Thought leaders in the islands met together in Waikiki in preparation for the International New Thought Alliance Congress, which comes up in July. It's nice to see this happening now. People are ready, not only there, but here and everywhere. People are receptive to the idea of expanding their own consciousness. They are ready to grow into awareness, into an understanding of the self and of life. And we have the tools to work with. We always have had them. Now we are seeing them come into practice.

I entitled my talk this morning with something that just moved through me when Dr. Bitzer was kind enough to invite me back in February, and I just felt like I wanted to speak about the spirit of Aloha. I looked up the word in the dictionary, because since I've heard it used, as you have too, in so many ways, I was certain there must be some real definition from a pure Hawaiian language. Let me share with you all the definitions I found.

Aloha first means love. Then affection, compassion, mercy, pity, kindness, charity, greeting, regard, sweetheart, loved one, beloved, loving, to love, to remember with affection; and if we add an exclamation point, it becomes greetings, hello, goodbye, farewell, and alas. Now, will that hold you for a while?

Do you know these words? Do you know what they mean? Isn't it remarkable that one word could mean so much? And how beautiful it is to have a word like that, that we can use so freely to express so many wonderful things. And did you notice basically what the main thread of thought was through all of that? The first word of love. That means a great deal to me. That's why I love the word Aloha. And I've had fun learning more about it and using it.

And now I find that it is a part of my vocabulary. When I answer the phone over there I do say it—"Aloha"—because I do mean "I love you, no matter who you are, and I want to say hello and allow you to feel that warmth and reception." It is nice when we can have words like that, that do have meaning. Of course, we have them, but we tend to use them so much—like "Hello, how are you? I'm fine. Great. How are the kids? Great." And that's it. And off you go into something else. And the words have come and gone without much real meaning about what the feeling is. So when we say this Aloha, we have a feeling behind the consciousness of love and caring.

I also thought it would be worthwhile looking up the actual meaning of the letters as they apply to the word Aloha. This will tell you about the consciousness of these loving people.

The first A stands for *akaha'i,* which is the Hawaiian meaning of kindness, to be expressed with tenderness.

The L stands for *lokahi,* the Hawaiian meaning for unity, to be expressed with harmony.

The O is for *olu'olu,* the Hawaiian meaning for agreeable, to be expressed with pleasantness.

The H, *ha'aha'a,* the Hawaiian meaning, humility, to be expressed with honesty.

And the final A, *ahonu'i,* Hawaiian meaning, patience, to be expressed with perseverance. Good advice.

Here I thought I had all the answers, fresh out of school, a little wet behind the ears. Then I go over there and find out they can teach me a whole lot more. And they're doing it. And we are sharing our cultures together now, and we are growing in a remarkable way.

I am dedicated to the growth of that little church. I am also grateful and appreciative to the remarkable people who created it eight years ago and who have maintained it in a very tiny community in sort of an out-of-the-way place. In the days before the tourist industry, which is now big there, it was very small; it was basically a fishing village. So we have some dedication of people who grasped the idea of the science of mind, and they made it work. And I am pleased to be an extension of that consciousness.

As I said before, we are the only ones. Somehow, there has been something there, working perfectly, that has perpetuated it; and now the time is right for our great growth and for our sharing of this beautiful teaching with so many wonderful people.

We have only one radio station on the Kona side of the island, and so I guess you could say it's a little bit of a monopoly. But that's all right. Everybody is very happy with it, and it is working very well. We have a little radio show. In January we decided that the time had come to put a little five-minute program on that station just before the noon news every day, Monday through Friday. And that was one of the wisest things we could have done, because people are coming from all over, as a result of just hearing five minutes of inspiration, five minutes of ideas for creative living. They are not being preached at. They are not being told anything they don't already know. But they are hearing it, perhaps, for the first time with a fresh idea or a new thought. And that's very exciting. It's one of my favorite things to do. From this, we are seeing what we knew was there, which is the desire and the need on the part of so many wonderful people to expand in their growth.

They call me and say, "I didn't know there was anyone else on this island who thought like I do." And that's something. You see, we all have, within us, the truth. We all have all of life. We do indeed operate in the One Mind; and we know it, but we don't always want to believe it.

We have allowed ourselves to condition ourselves away from trust in that inner knowing. And that's all right. We have that other side of us. We are in a polarity of life, and we have the ability and the right to move through the cycle, based on our thought and our own choice.

Until such time as we are ready to grow, we will go through some of the growing experience—which we sometimes label as being "unpleasant" or "painful" or "bad" or even "evil."

Aloha turns out to be a preparation for something that I have been dealing with for a long time. I didn't realize it until this morning, and I'm glad that it came through—which it always does—in time so that I could share it.

Aloha obviously starts with the letter A. I've been fascinated for some time about the words that begin with the letter A; and I found out some years ago that what I call "The Pathway to Fulfillment" is directed entirely by words which express our emotions with words that begin with the letter A. And today it dawned on me that Aloha is the first one. I had always had another one in mind. I am sure you are already thinking of all the different words there are. There are so many positive words that we use. But if we had a seminar workshop going right now, I would throw this out to you and let you work on it for a while and see if you could come up with the first emotional state of mind that begins with an A that sets us off unto a path of fulfillment with people. This has to do now with relationships—which is what life is all about. I can hear you all thinking now—but I'm going to save you a lot of energy and I will tell you.

The very first word—or the first thought—that we would like to see come into our consciousness with respect to meeting someone, is simply: "acknowledgement." I know that many of you are already into "acceptance" and "appreciation" and all those, but there is a key here and I bring it to your attention because it's a great discovery that I have made in my life, and I love teaching it, and that is: the very first thing I must do as I meet each one of you— and I'm meeting you now—is to acknowledge that you are here. You will notice that there is absolutely no effort whatsoever in that. I have not had to make any decisions about you. I have not made any judgments or evaluations or opinions. I have simply acknowledged that you are there—and I'm here—and that is the key to our having a fulfilling relationship.

Now, I might wander off this path from time to time, but if I return to the very first step after I have greeted you with "Aloha," I will acknowledge you simply as a fellow human being. What a beautiful thing to do.

Now, you try this. It's a little challenging because, you see, your mind and mine have been conditioned for years to jump far ahead to various degrees of judgment.

The second step is acceptance, which I think most people feel they want to give. That is the "I want to accept you." But we first have to acknowledge. After acceptance, to further ourselves in the relationship, we must simply have approval. Now, right here I want to stop and explain something because, as we go down this path, I can hear your minds working like mine used to. And that was that we are getting caught up in the outward appearance of what we are seeing in another person. And I am not really talking about that. I'm asking you to see through the appearance to the reality of this fellow human being. That is how you can acknowledge and accept and approve the reality of what they are doing or saying or acting like. Whether they are accepting or rejecting, it makes no difference here. We are talking about *your* experience, which is the only experience you can have—the experience of your emotions, your feelings, your life, that you and you alone control. And so now you give new insight to your mind by allowing it to simply acknowledge life; and there is life expressed in a beautiful form of a fellow human being, regardless of what he looks like and what he sounds like. We have heard this before, and we'll hear it again, until we get it right. Right? Okay.

Now, after approval comes appreciation. At this point we are really starting to get some feeling. We are allowing ourselves to flow freely with and through the life that exists in and around all of us—the One Life. You see, I can appreciate you regardless of what you are doing or what you are saying. And you can do that too. But it takes a little work. Perhaps you will want to use these as guidelines to direct yourself in a new course of relationships. If you really feel that people are good, that life is okay, that you just haven't really become completely centered on this path, and you know it is there and you see other people doing it, there are some wonderful directions. And it begins in our mind with our thought. As we add feelings and beliefs and convictions to these things, they manifest in our life. It all begins with that very first idea. If the first idea is neutral, we can't get into too much trouble, can we? It happens only when we put a condition on the thought, which is, of course, some kind of evaluation or opinion or judgment.

We've still got three more A's to go here. Isn't that amazing? Could there be so much more? Sure.

After appreciation is admiration. How nice to admire someone, to have reached that level of consciousness with life! Again, regardless of what's being done. There are two more, and a lot of people would like to challenge these somewhat. But I believe in them. I've seen them work.

The next one is adoration. Would you believe that, after you could reach that high in appreciation of someone, there could be still another feeling?

This is one that there could be an entire seminar on. It is affection. And if you can express affection for a fellow human being without any fear, without any guilt—just honest affection—you have arrived at one of the highest states of consciousness I believe you can attain and still have your feet on the ground.

I call Religious Science the practical religion. That's what appealed to me many years ago. I had the wonderful pleasure of meeting and knowing Ernest Holmes when I was twelve years old. That was the first seed planted. And that was at the Wilshire-Ebell Theater. I was greatly inspired by the warmth and the sincerity; but above all was the fact that I could now do something. I had gotten rid of the ideas of fear and guilt—at least a great deal of them. And, of course, as a young person, I didn't have that much, but there was enough there because I had had some different training. And then there was a way to do something about it, and that was treatment, affirmation, and retraining of the mind—that mind that you had already given up to someone else or to something else over all these years, because you believed what you were told, and it may or may not have been correct for you.

If it was not, you were operating on a false belief system; and that is what we need to get in touch with a little bit. There is no judgment on this. There is no need to blame anybody or any *thing*. Whether you want to admit it or not, you have got it your own way. You are the one that gets to say yes or no in your consciousness. And now is the time when we can be very consciously aware of that choice. And we have the right to say, "No, I do not want to do that any longer," or, "No, I refuse to be the victim," or, "No, I do not want to be used any longer."

We give up a great deal to other people. They don't take it from us. They invite it with a very strong personality and their need to dominate. But *we* have to give it up. If we do, that has been our decision, and we can always get it right back. You see, there's always a way out.

One of the greatest lessons you hear about today—and I'm totally convinced that it's absolutely the most effective thing in the world—is to get your conscious mind right into the now, totally into the now. When you are here, mentally and physically, there can be no problem in life. The problems occur when we allow ourselves to drift into the past which no longer exists, or into the future which has not gotten here yet. Neither exists. And I know—because I've sat in an audience—what you're saying and thinking. I even have to watch this, because even as I am talking to you, my mind has the ability to race ahead or flash back. If I do that, I've allowed myself a certain sense of separation. And I no longer choose to be separated from my source, which is God, which is an Infinite Creative Intelligence that is ever-present, which you have heard. But isn't it the truth?

Doesn't it make sense that a Creative Power in this universe is indeed available to everyone? And the joy of that is that each of us not only can use it but that each of us *is* using it. It is not something out "there" that we've got to earn and that we've got to "get to." That's not it at all. That has been the misconception. What it is, then, is what is already active within us. It is a total, natural, harmonious, healing consciousness, an ever-evolving expansion of the idea of love, God's love, that must manifest. It must express Itself, and It does. And It does so, remarkably well, in you and me as what we at this time know to be the highest form of that expression. It's quite an honor. I would much rather be a human being than anything else on this earth. And the reason is that I have the awareness of all of the other and I have the ability to communicate with it. That allows me, therefore, to enjoy and participate in life fully.

My, the morning goes quickly when you're having fun. I've had fun. I know you've had fun too. It's wonderful when we can get together and spend a precious little time to share ideas, thoughts, which indeed are things. Thoughts in our life are the things that make our life. And the great Polynesian culture, known as the Huna, many years ago, understood all these principles and demonstrated instantaneous healing. They understood the higher self, and they knew that it was within. And now we are rediscovering that for our own self, for our own culture, and for our own time. So we can be grateful that we can appreciate the gift of the Polynesian and his beautiful language and the wonderful loving word Aloha.

Aloha nui loa. Mahalo.

Reverend David Bair is minister-teacher of the Kona Community Church of Religious Science on the "Big Island" in the State of Hawaii.

Before his ministry, Reverend Bair spent 16 years in the insurance industry as a sales manager and consultant.

Reverend Bair was appointed to the Kona church in 1978, after completing his ministerial training at the Science of Mind Center in Glendale, California under the direction of Dr. Leo Fishbeck. In addition to the time he devotes to his church duties, he presents a daily radio program called, "Ideas for Creative Living."

The talk, "The Spirit of Aloha," was given by Reverend Bair at the Hollywood, California Church of Religious Science, when he was there as guest speaker on May 6, 1979.

CHAPTER THREE

It is not the place, nor the condition, but the mind alone that can make anyone happy or miserable.

—L'Estrange

Failure is Hard Work

Dr. Raymond C. Barker

Good morning.

And I would like to say—when I get this mike adjusted, all right, I think we are in order, I hope we are still on the air. I am a threat to any form of mechanism; the worst thing anybody can do is to hand me a hammer or a screwdriver; they are lethal; they're the end of everything.

I'd like to say for those who are not with us—that are listening by radio—this is Raymond Charles Barker speaking to you from Alice Tully Hall in New York City, and it is with joy that I am back on the job again. And I expect to be your speaker every Sunday morning until at least the first of January, and I think maybe longer. So, you might get ready for it.

Now, this morning I have a topic I like, so I say to the radio audience, don't turn off, you're going to hear something great, I think. The topic is "Failure is Hard Work."

All right, we'll talk about that later. Now, what are we going to talk about here?

24

There is a universal goodness. There still is a living God. I say that because it takes a bit of faith and remembrance, many times, to realize it, to know it again. There is a livingness, a creativeness, there is That which creates lovingly out of Itself. And we are in It and we are of It. We forget it often, but it still remains so.

Let's be still and take this as a meditation and a treatment so that we know deep within ourselves—and I'll do it in the first person for you, then it becomes your own:

I am immersed in an eternal goodness, an eternal creative Spirit, Mind, Power. I am in all that life is and all that love is and all that beauty is, and this is the Living Spirit Almighty. My subconscious mind accepts it. And it is so.

Now, to our lesson for the day, "Failure is Hard Work."

I think that I should start a talk on such a subject with a definition of both success and failure, because we have taken both words greatly out of context and we have made them into something that really isn't so.

Success in this country—and I'm sure in others—is pretty much premised upon how much money you have, how much money you make, where you live, what you do, et cetera. Now, to me, that is not success. It's an angle of success, yes, but it is not success. To me, success is when you are doing that which is productive, with ease and with joy and with a minimum of frustration. So we select these great men and women of industry and all the rest and we say, "Well, they're successful." Then we look down and say, "Well, I'm not." Don't be too sure of that at all. Any person is a success who is productive, who enjoys what he or she is doing, who is glad to have the compensation for same, and who has some joy in living. To me, that is success.

Now let's talk about failure. Again, we have made the whole thing of failure a matter of money. So we speak of a man or a woman and say, "Well, but they are a failure."

Don't be too sure at all. They might be failures according to the standards of the world, just as we have seen that success is not a matter of the standards of the world. To me, a failure is the individual who probably has never in his or her life known creativity, who has never known the joy of producing, who has never had a sense of worth and a belief in himself or in herself as being a spiritual potential.

I know that from the viewpoint of psychology and psychotherapy a great portion of so-called failures can be explained by their area of birth, the type of family into which they came, the education or lack of it which they had, et cetera.

Years ago a teacher told me, "When you're dealing with psychology"—of which we have no negative thought at all—"the one thing to remember is that psychology explains the problem but only our metaphysical teaching can heal it." If any of you have notebooks, put that down. Psychology can explain a problem or the causes of it way back. But psychology does not heal; it only explains.

Now, the psychological causes behind failure of a man or a woman are as infinite in number as there are people that fail, and psychologically these things are right. What I mean is that they are so. Well, what are you going to do about it?

An early teacher we had—this is back in the 1980s—Malinda Kramer, out on the west coast in San Francisco, read in the newspaper that a very famous teacher of those days, Emma Curtis Hopkins, was coming in to give a course of lessons on healing. This woman, Malinda Kramer, who had been a chronic invalid for years—a walking drug store of the period—went and heard Mrs. Hopkins. After the lecture she went home.

Her husband heard her puttering around, and he said, "Well, dear, what are you doing? Look, you're pouring all your medicines down the sink!"

She said, "Yes, I know."

Then he said, "What are you going to *do*?"

She answered, "I have decided to get well!"

She never had another sick day until she died thirty years later. Now, that doesn't mean that you should go home and do it, unless it fits you.

In my apartment, you wouldn't find much in the medicine cabinet to throw away. Very little. A package of Band Aids and a few things. Oh, always aspirins—because I have guests. And when I take the bottle out and hand it to them with a glass, they say, "My, this bottle is dirty and old." I say, "Well, I've had it for fifteen years."

Now to come back. I'm not speaking about the virtue of having or not having a medicine cabinet filled with medicine. I am merely saying, here is a woman who decided not to be sick any longer and had the emotional and mental constitution to follow through on it by believing that her health was God in action. And so she was well. And then later she began to teach.

Coming back. The failure can be made into a success, and it has nothing to do with age, situation, environment, or anything else. It has to do, ladies and gentlemen, with being happy.

I've often quoted to you one of our great English metaphysical teachers. And when he lectured in this country, as well as in England, and people would ask to see him and he would see them, his first question was not, "What is wrong?" His first question was, "What will make you happy?" And often the person sitting across the desk would say, "I didn't come for that! I want to tell you all about my arthritis," or, "I want to tell you all about my cataracts," or, "I want to tell you all about my sore knee."

And he'd sit back and say, "What will make you happy?" —because he knew if he could give them an incentive for being happy, the rest would take care of itself.

So, the key to success is happiness.

Oh, yes, it takes intellectual ability. In many instances it takes real genius. But, really, deep underneath, unhappy people don't make much of a contribution to the world. No. Our basic teachers past and present have always been happy people.

I knew Ernest Holmes very well. I knew Charles Fillmore very well. These were happy people. Yes. Now, you're going to say, "Well, but they died." Well, who won't? I mean, you know, let's not kid ourselves.

Coming back to a nicer subject, both of these men were happy men, happy people, creative, dynamic, happy. You're going to say, "Were they rich?" No, because they didn't need it. That wasn't their goal. You see, Ernest Holmes, or I, or anyone else who's good in his field, we, in the commercial world today, could have made millions. I could have sold books or life insurance, and I could today be whatever is the greatest symbol of money success. Luckily I didn't want to do it. I wanted to do what I'm doing.

Now, am I broke? Far from it. So you don't have to take up a special collection for a new roof on the parsonage. There isn't a parsonage.

Now, to come back. Success has a great deal to do with joy as well as with productivity. Yes. Producing something. But producing it in a consciousness that is basically creative. Now, you're going to say, "Well, who's happy all the time?" I agree, no one is. I don't want to worry about that. I only worry about the people that are unhappy too much of the time. And many are unhappy too much of the time.

People say, "Well, Dr. Barker, aren't you happy all the time?" My answer is, "No. But I'm happy 98 per cent of the time. And that's all that for me is necessary." They might say, "Oh, but didn't Jesus say we are all to be perfect?" Well, if he did he was wrong. Oh, I thought I'd get a reaction to that. Well, all right, but don't go home and tell your friends what I just said. He may have said it or he may not have said it. We don't know really what this man did say. We have great respect for him.

Coming back, no one is happy all the time. And no one is unhappy all the time that has the wit and wisdom to know that there's a way out of this and a way to be happy.

It's hard work to be a failure, yes. Do you realize the hours, days, weeks, and months of worry? Of fear? Of trying to find self-justification in the newspapers? The situations? The politics of the day? Whatsoever. The need to self-justify failure. But, you didn't cause it. "The world did it, the government did it, the state did it, the city did it, somebody did it." If you're a man you can blame it on your wife; if you're a woman you can blame it on your husband; if you're a child you can blame it on the parents; so on it goes, endless, endless circle. But always someone breaks it.

Every psychological study of Abraham Lincoln shows that this man should never have been a success. He was born in the wrong place, he had no money, he struggled to get his education instead of staying home running a farm and marrying a farm lady and having children who would help to run the farm. You see, in those days farmers had to have children because you had to have hired help that you didn't have to pay. He should have been a failure, but he wasn't, you see. The whole explanation was there.

This could be true of many people—not just him—the people who, despite what the world brought to their door, knew that lovely statement of Jesus, "Greater is he that is within me than he that is within the world." For the indwelling mind, perfect in its action, knows what to do, reveals what to do—and you follow it through and all is well. A classic statement: "Greater is he that is within me than he that is within the world."

Does it take hard work to fail? It sure does. Does it take

hard work to be successful? It most certainly does. There's no life on this planet that is eternally easy. You're going to say, "Well, but look at the people who were born with a golden spoon in their mouth." Well, look at them. They are not overly happy unless they are creative; unless, again, they have created their own happiness at a different economic level than yours may be. So it is so easy to sit back and say, "They have all the breaks and I didn't get any." Then create your own. I had to create mine. Yes, I had to create my own breaks. But I knew I could do it. And there, you see, the average person today is lost.

So many people today no longer believe they can do it. Don't you be among their number! Don't you rest with the multitudes saying, "Poor me. I wish somebody out there somewhere, that man in the sky"—or some other symbol—"would only come in and help me." And all the time there is that great wisdom of the Greeks, "Know thyself." And so the great guy in the sky, if there is one, and I don't think there is, but if there were one, will not come down and take care of you. But you have within you the equipment to do it yourself. "Greater is he that is within me than he that is within the world."

When you read your newspapers later today, it takes a bit of thinking, knowing, what I have just said, and all the rest. But there is no easy route to either success or failure. It's more fun to be a success. But the failure people don't see that. There is greater joy in living fully and richly—and I'm not talking about money here at all—there is greater joy.

Some years ago—and I couldn't even now tell you who it was—a woman in my office said to me, "Dr. Barker, I have retired and I'm living on social security and some savings, and I am so happy." I said, "Isn't that wonderful? Because 99 per cent of the people who sit in this office and tell me about living on social security and their savings are bitter and unpleasant.''

You see, your grandfather, wherever he may be, if he's able to look down, is thinking, "My God, and I worked so damn hard and I never had social security." So this woman—I literally hugged her. I said, "You are wonderful! Here is a person that's happy." She said, "Now I can do what I want to do when I want to do it." And I said, "That's wonderful. Isn't that great?" She said, "It certainly is." And so, she was a success. In money, I don't know what she had or didn't have. She was moderately dressed, lived at a moderate address; but I'll bet she lived clean and lived well—and lived happy!

So I think the greatest single factor between failure and success is "Are you happy?" And if you're not, what are you going to do about it? Sit in your misery? Or, find the way from within? Because it's there.

The Divine Mind has not left you. It always indwells you with all of its activity. And it is always saying, "Look unto me instead of the problem, and I will give you the solution."

Years ago we had a writer in our field—gone now; only old, old timers would know him. He used to speak for us. One of his favorite topics was, "Joy is an Inside Job." And this was a happy man. All you had to do was look at him and you could tell he was happy. "Joy is an Inside Job." People would listen and they'd laugh at his jokes. And if you think I'm corny, you should have heard *him.* At any rate, they'd go out and say, "Wasn't it wonderful?" And they'd go back home and be just as miserable as ever. Oh, he was wonderful, gave a great talk.

"But look at me. Here I am. And look at my little income and look at my little living conditions and look at this and look at that." And, "If only my Uncle Harry would die and leave me some money." It wouldn't solve a thing.

No Barker ever left me a cent, and I thank God now that they didn't. It might have stopped me on my way. It might have also made my life a little nicer at the time, but we won't go into that.

Now, to come back to the lesson. Yes, joy, love, beauty— these are factors that if you have them, you are a success. And without them, you are—I will put it this way: temporarily a failure.

There is no finality to failure, you can always come back. You can always rebuild, you can always get a new idea. There's always a way out of any negative. We forget it. You see, that's what these great early teachers always were telling their people. The sick *can* be healed; the unhappy *can* be made glad; the poor *can* be prospered; because the action of God, that Great Mind, is still in business. That's what these early teachers told us—from Quimby, Mrs. Eddy, right down to the present, Hopkins and all—that a negative situation is always temporary to the person who rejects it and sees its opposite. And we are the people who are seeking the opposites, because they're there: life, spirit, love, joy, inspiration, prosperity, peace—all of these things are. But you have to find them through an inward route, "The Inside Job."

All right, then, that's failure, and that's also success.

This is a good talk you heard this morning, and I'm not joking. I know when I give a good one and I know when I don't.

Dr. Raymond Charles Barker is one of the brightest lights in the New Thought movement.

He was originally trained at the Unity School of Christianity in Lee's Summit and was ordained by Charles Fillmore in 1940. Later he changed to Religious Science and has been in that ministry for 35 years.

Dr. Barker is one of the most respected and admired of the RSI ministers. He is known and loved from coast to coast by students of New Thought, through church lectures, radio sermons, writings, and personal contact. His good humor and quick wit are legend; and his love for mankind is apparent in his messages which are always on the "up-beat."

Previous to assuming the ministry of the New York First Church, from which he is retiring, he was co-minister of the San Francisco Church in 1944.

Books which Dr. Barker has authored are, "Treat Yourself to Life," "Power of Decision," "Science of Successful Living," "You are Invisible," and, with Ernest Holmes, "Richer Living."

The many years Dr. Barker has given to the RSI ministry attest to his devotion to the teaching which so greatly inspired him. In addition to his duties as a minister, he was RSI President from 1954 to 1957 and International New Thought Alliance President from 1943 to 1946. It is anticipated that Dr. Barker will continue writing and lecturing after his retirement from the New York First Church.

Students of metaphysics will discover a wealth of information, instruction, and inspiration by delving into Dr. Barker's many recorded talks and published writings.

The talk, "Failure is Hard Work," was delivered by Dr. Barker at Alice Tully Hall, Lincoln Center, in New York City on August 6, 1978.

CHAPTER FOUR

As long as you are true to your Christ Self, as long as you are true to the God Self within you, you can't possibly experience anything that is less than Perfection, or less than Godly.

—Bonaccorso

Don't Neglect Your Divinity

Reverend Anthony Bonaccorso

"I'm only human." I don't know how many times I've said that. I'm sure you've said it too. "I'm only human." I know what I used to mean when I said it. After these past few days of preparing for today's subject, I know what I'll mean from now on when I say, "I'm only human."

This morning, I want to answer the question of how human you are and how human I am. I'd like to begin by stating the conclusion which I reached after asking myself that question. The conclusion is metaphysical and has been taught in metaphysical churches throughout this country for more than a hundred years. As a matter of fact, the concepts involved here were taught by Jesus some 2,000 years ago.

Simply stated, these concepts are that I'm not very human at all, thank heaven; I am Divine, I am totally and completely Spirit, I am absolute and unconditioned Spirit, I am perfect, I am complete, I am Love expressing Itself as love. I also know that I am the Christ, that the Christ is the man that God created.

I believe that from the "beginning" there was a perfect God and nothing else—a loving God that was perfect in every way, complete, whole. And that's all that there was—and is. Therefore, believing that, my conclusion was then so easy to come to: The only thing that there was to create anything from, in the beginning, was this God substance, and God created from Himself, man. Since God is perfect, that which He creates must also be perfect. When God created man, He created the perfect man, or the Christ man.

However, I also believe that because man was born into this human world, man takes on human conditions. I, as man, assume human thinking. Now, if I took on the right kind of human thinking, that would be one thing. But, unfortunately, I, as man, participate in a process of thinking which is not quite so human.

What is your definition of the word "human?" Your definition may be rather negative. I like to think that the word "human" is derived from the word "humane" which to me means "kindly." The "human" observes nature with love and adoration. That's my sense of humanness now. It wasn't previously.

Therefore, now I can be human, you see. I can take on humanness and know that it is the Christ living its Life in a human way, and I can feel good about that.

But before, when I was saying, "I'm only human," I meant that I was taking on the *appearance* of that human aspect which was rather negative and limited.

"But what do you expect of me? I'm only human!" We've all said it. And that statement forgave us for doing things in a limited human way.

Alexander Pope said, "To err is human; to forgive, divine." When we look at the second part of that statement, we can ask, "Who does the forgiving?" We know that God does not forgive. We can say that in a metaphysical church. Everyone who is a member of the Church of Religious

Science or who has had classes or who understands meta-physics can understand that God does not forgive. And I can shout this to hundreds of people out there in the human world and they wouldn't understand my meaning. I think I would really turn them off.

God does not forgive. Metaphysicians know this. God does not forgive, because there's nothing to forgive. The man-world wishes God to forgive. But in order for God to forgive, in order for this Supreme Intelligence to be capable of forgiving, It would first have to understand what there is to forgive. God can't do that because He can't under-stand "sin." He can't understand failings. In order for God to understand a failing, He must be part of the failing. In order for God to understand the "sin," He's got to be part of the sin. And God is not part of sin. Just as light cannot recognize the darkness, God cannot recognize sin. There is no sin in God. So there's nothing to forgive. Who does the forgiving? Each individual does; you must forgive yourself.

The Christ within you is revealed when you and I under-stand the true nature of God. The nature of God is the benevolent, all loving, all accepting, all encompassing, spiritual Something which I touch whenever I close my eyes and move into prayer. And It is unmistakable.

Dr. Richelieu, the minister of the Religious Science Church at Redondo Beach, California, said it beautifully two years ago at an Asilomar meeting. He said, "If there's one thing you know, it must be that you are alive. When you close your eyes and you think, what is the thing that you know beyond a shadow of a doubt? You know that you're alive."

And I know that too. I know that I am alive. And so the thing that I know that I am is this Christ within me, this Divinity within me that lives forever and ever and ever, from eternity to eternity it lives. I'm not "human" then in

the sense that I feel that humanness ends and Divinity begins at some point. I don't live that way. And I won't live
that way. I am really and truly a Divine child. I live from
that point of view.

Jesus is a beautiful concept for me. Jesus represents
God's idea of man. God, being perfect and complete and
whole, Almighty—not sometimes mighty—must, as It becomes what It creates, become the Christ man, never losing
any of the verities of life, never losing the Reality. So you
are that Perfection. You are that Power. You are that Mind,
that All-Knowing Mind. You are the Christ man.

Now, if there is ever a sin that we've committed, it is the
sin of being born into an Adam-world which believes in
lack and limitation. I know that lack and limitation are
what we sometimes give strength and power to.

We believe, in Religious Science, that there is a law of
cause and effect—a law which responds to us according to
our belief. Jesus knew this when he said, "It is done unto
you as you believe." This is the law that we live by. And,
unfortunately, we give tremendous strength to things that
are not Reality, to things that are temporal, to things that
will change. Remember, God's Reality *never* changes. And
if something changes, we know that it is not Reality. We
know that it is fact, perhaps. It's fact, but it's not permanent, and, therefore, it's not Reality. You see, *facts* change.
The fact that you may be experiencing a cold today will
change.

The fact that you are healthy will *never* change. The
Reality that you are pure and whole and complete and that
you are total health—that will never change. That's Reality.

We give power and strength, as human beings, to false
beliefs that have been put into mind by whom? Who knows?
People, through their fear and through their lack of faith,

have given power to the idea that a germ gives a cold, to the idea that an abnormal growth can't be stopped. We should not give those ideas any authority at all.

Let's explain this business of a condition in health and see whether it makes sense to you. The moment an individual understands that he is responsible for everything that happens to him—whether that be in the body of his health or in the body of his affairs—that individual can take charge of his life.

Let's look at how this works. I hope that by now you have accepted that you are the Christ. I can accept it for you, but I can't live it for you. I accept this for you and so I know that you are accepting it yourself to a greater and greater degree. I accept the Christ in you. If you like that concept and you are suffering from a cold right now, you may be saying, "All I have to do is know that God doesn't have a cold?—that I am total health? —that God inspires me? —that God is my life? So why isn't this cold leaving me?"

I wish to address myself to this. If in Truth, deep within yourself—in that place within you where you level with yourself—you accept the truth about your health, if you totally accept that you are health personified, then that cold, that congestion, dissolves immediately, and we have an instantaneous healing. All healing is instantaneous. But sometimes it takes a little time for the body to catch up with the mental acceptance.

It is one thing to say, "Yes, I like what Tony is saying," or, "I like what I've heard, I don't accept this cold any longer. Cold, begone! I accept only the health of God."

But has the *consciousness* that accepted that cold *really* changed? Because, you see, when you entered into that cold experience in the first place, you were giving power, or authority, to the "cold" concept. As soon as you give power to it, it is born within you, and then it has to do whatever humanity says that a cold ordinarily does.

We have all kinds of colds, all kinds of congestion, all kinds of influenza; therefore, depending on what you gave truth to, or depending on what you gave power to, that's what you are going to experience—according to your belief. You can shorten that period of belief, you can shorten that period of experience, depending upon your faith. If your faith is total, the cold will go like the snap of the fingers. Sometimes we get healed of a cold instantly, but two weeks later it returns. And we ask, "Why did I catch a cold again?" The answer is, you *did* have an instantaneous healing but it wasn't established. And what I want to do is *establish* in my life the Divinity principle, the idea that Tony Bonaccorso is a Divine idea, is the Christ idea, being given birth in the human experience, and experiencing the Divine in the human.

Let's talk about something not as common as a cold. Let's talk about a physical growth. Again, remember, as there are many kinds of colds, there are many kinds of growths. Scientists have said that there are some growths which are O.K. growths, and there are some growths which are not O. K. growths. There are growths which have been given names that cause the strong to tremble. We are not even going to mention those names in here. Again, look at what happens. As a human, if you give power to the human and you experience a growth, there had to be an initiating thought within you. I don't necessarily believe that it is a conscious thought within you creating the condition, because our Science of Mind textbook says that 90 per cent of all the physical illnesses which we experience have not been specifically thought by each of us in a conscious way, but they somehow or other have been given strength, have been given power—there's been an authority given to the thing, to the disease, to the illness, to the imperfection, in a subconscious or unconscious way.

Simply by coming into this world and becoming part of

the human experience, we take on the human limitation. We take on the belief, the belief of the human. Once you hear, understand, and accept, that you are perfect Divine man, you will be free from limited human belief. And, you no longer have to be subject to disease as a power. You no longer are subject to that, and so you can release yourself from it. But you can't do this just by saying, "Ah, it sounds great on Sunday hearing Tony say that I don't have to be subject to disease or illness, and now I won't be." You must do it. You must do your mental work. You must do this yourself. I can't do it for you. I can spiritually embrace you, and you can feel the power of that embrace because it comes from the Father within me; but *you* have to do the mental work that is necessary, and say, "Yes, I am the Christ made manifest as the individual"—and you add your own name to that.

God having only Itself to work with said, "I'll make man, and I'll make it kind." And when He made it, He said, "It is good." And it was, and it is, and it always will be. You have the choice of living with that perfect creation and accepting the glory of it, and of living in your paradise, living in your heaven now. You have the right of choice, because we were given free will. And you can choose not to experience the Divine experience but to experience the human experience. Therefore, when the growth comes along, maybe it wasn't your fault at all in consciousness. However, perhaps you didn't work hard enough to get rid of race belief, this hypnotism which we have accepted over the years in the subconscious.

Let's go back to the growth. If this is your experience, there must be something that you gave power to, something that you said "yes" to, something you affirmed that is providing the growth experience, the thing that is *not* needed by your body. However, at the moment you realize

God did not create the growth, you experience a healing. The strength of this thought established in your mind will determine the degree to which this growth leaves your body.

Do you have a great acceptance of the Divine idea? And is that acceptance firmly established? If it is, you won't see that growth again. But if you stop believing that you are the Christ in human form, at that moment you will experience lack, limitation, the growth, or whatever.

As long as you are true to your Christ Self, as long as you are true to the God Self within you, you can't possibly experience anything that is less than Perfection, or less than Godly.

We are told how to do this over and over again. I was told how to do this, as a child.

I saw the great metaphysical teaching, as a youngster, when someone gave me a pen wiper as a gift. There were three little metal monkeys sitting on top of the pen wiper. One of the monkeys had his hands over his eyes, another had his hands over his ears, and the other had his hands over his mouth. And I said, "Oh, gee, isn't that cute?" I had that thing for a long time and I've seen those three monkeys for a long time without realizing that those monkeys were teaching me a great lesson which I really needed to learn in order to live the Christ life right here and right now. It didn't dawn on me until I was a metaphysician that those monkeys told it all: "See no evil, hear no evil, speak no evil."

And if I follow that advice then I would no longer be subject to the human negative experience. I would be subject to the human kindly, the human positive, the Christ-in-the-human experience. Because, after all, in the beginning, God—perfect, complete, Divine. And out of this Substance, this Essence, you and I were made, because that's the only Essence, the only Thing that there ever was. And this *Something* created, by becoming that which It created. And It became You and It became Me, and this always will be.

Therefore, I don't have to worry about being human right now and losing my life when I arrive at that place where I have to make my transition. I don't have to worry about that, because I've always been in the Mind of God. I have always been part of that Substance, that Essence, that Something. I've always been That, and I always will be That. And knowing this, deep within myself, it takes away fear and does away with guilt. It does away with all this negative stuff that I don't need to experience. I don't need to experience it. And so I don't.

I also know that my body is the body of God. And the body of my affairs also expresses this wholeness. And when I see no evil, hear no evil, and speak no evil, I don't experience the bad facts of life. I don't experience the evil. I experience only the Good. I experience only the Godly.

So, welcome to a place where we experience Paradise. Welcome to a place where we teach this positive way of thinking. Welcome to a place where we unashamedly extend our arms, our hearts, and our minds to you and say, welcome. Welcome to the Christ. It is in me. It is in you. And when you recognize it in me, it's because you are first recognizing it in you.

Reverend Anthony Bonaccorso is currently the minister for the Salem, Oregon Woodland Chapel First Church of Religious Science. Previous to that, he had the Ukiah, California church, which he founded.

The business and professional background of Reverend Bonaccorso is quite extensive. He spent 16 years as a high school speech and drama instructor; he owned and operated a restaurant for 4 years and an employment agency for 3 years; he has had varied sales experience:

automotive, real estate, and educational courses. For one year he was associated with the Napoleon Hill Academy in Oakland, California where he taught "The Science of Personal Achievement."

Studies for the ministry were completed by Reverend Bonaccorso at the Monterey, California Church of Religious Science, with Dr. Oscar M. Pitcock.

The lesson by Reverend Bonaccorso printed here is from a talk given by him on March 25, 1979 at the Salem, Oregon church.

CHAPTER FIVE

Do you want to be justified or healed? You can't be both. Do you want to be justified about how mistreated you were, how unhappy you are? Don't try to be justified of your injustices, be healed of them.

—Costa

Get Out of God's Way

Reverend Tom Costa

I am doing a Scripture reading from the Book of Revelation which I don't do very often. In Revelation, verse 8, it says, "I know thy works; behold, I have set before thee an open door, and no man can shut it."

Nobody shuts our doors except ourselves. Nobody opens our doors except ourselves. The doors are already open.

I'll bet you thought I am going to talk about April Fools' Day today. Well, in a way I am. In a way I will be talking about how we fool ourselves. If you can apply it to yourself, you will get the whole point, because if you are having a problem, you are fooling yourself. You are fooling yourself if you believe that you are not an individualized expression of God.

There is nothing wrong with God. So April Fools' Day is saying, "Hey, I don't believe in myself. The joke is on me. Ha ha." Except that you're not laughing.

44

When we say that our good is right here right now, do we know what that means? The Book of John says that it is the Father's good pleasure to give you the kingdom. Okay. How much are you going to take? I say, "Bring your own containers. It's up to you."

When we say, "Our good is here and now," do we know what that means? Jesus said, "The kingdom of heaven is already at hand." That means right now. And sometimes when you are looking for a helping hand, it is right at the end of your arm.

Religious Science is a Do-It-Yourself religion. Nobody can do it for you except you. "No one can give peace to you except you," as Emerson said. But what is it that prevents us from doing that?

It sounds kind of flowery when we say, "Our good is at hand, abundance is at hand, health is at hand, love is at hand." We hear those words and believe them for about two minutes. What stops us from believing that our good is at hand? We can say, "I have opened the door and only I can shut it." Why do we shut it? The answer can be found in two words: "obstruction" and "delay;" that is to say, a belief in obstruction and a belief in delay.

False belief is the only thing that is keeping you separated from your good. If you believe that you are unworthy of it—which is a belief in obstruction—it is a blasphemy upon the God Self within you. If you condemn yourself, you are thereby obstructing your good.

I like to think of God as having a divine hose pouring His love and joy upon you. If we step on His hose, it kinks. Then the hose is in a state of being useless. It's in a state of kinking. I'd call it "kinking thinking," if you are the one who is kinking the divine hose. It's like stepping on your garden hose and preventing the water from coming through. That's what we sometimes do with ourselves, that's what we do with our minds, we step on our own selves. We like to think that other people are responsible for the stoppage. Not true. I don't see anyone here in chains other than mental ones.

The word "obstruct" according to Webster means "to choke, to clog, to oppose, to retard, to impede." Do you recognize any of those when applying it to your good? "Delay" means "put off to some future time, suspend, cause to move slowly."

I grew up in a religion that says I should be rewarded in the kingdom of heaven. Well, I don't hold that belief any more. I am rewarded by the laws of my own mind, right here and right now. My hell is right here; my heaven is right here. What's after is after. I am not going to eat the icing and miss the cake. We are entitled to all of the good in the world.

Does anyone here have a hangup about money? I think that anyone who has been in Religious Science for more than one year who is not abundant and who blames other people for malpractice for becoming abundant should not be here. You can find religious philosophies teaching that you are unworthy of your good.

There is enough good to go around. We talk about the energy crisis. Do you know what the latest thing is that we are short of? There's a shortage of caviar! That, to me, is the epitome of shortages. It's very interesting that when we had a gasoline shortage in 1974, according to "them" there was also a shortage of paprika, the red stuff that you never know what to do with. As long as you believe in obstruction you won't get gasoline. As long as you believe in delay of your good, that's exactly where you are. If you don't change what you are, you stay right where you are. Obstruct and delay, that's what we frequently do to ourselves.

If anybody has a problem within, it is due to those two

words: obstruction and delay. Every time someone says "Pray that my brother is GOING to be better," it has the effect of delaying the brother's chances of being better right now. We don't believe in that "going to be" stuff, or in that "will be" stuff, or in that "put off till tomorrow" stuff. What's wrong with today? I pray that your brother is all right RIGHT NOW. I don't pray that he's GOING TO BE all right. If I did that, it might take ten years for him to be all right.

It's similar to a situation about a real estate man I know. He could not close a deal. Everything went along great until the bottom line was to be signed. He couldn't sign it. He felt unworthy of the commission. So they would have to bring in a real pro, a closer, to sign the contract. In looking at someone like that—someone who can't close a deal—you see that there is a belief in obstruction. It is a belief that "you're not worthy of the commission." I believe that when you do your work you are entitled to receive just compensation for that work. I don't believe in doing work and not getting justly paid for it. So a belief in obstruction is the reason a person cannot close deals. That's why there are pros; they know that they are worthy of that just compensation.

Many times we have the "also ran." But, you know, "almost" doesn't count except in horseshoes. We have people who almost, but never quite make it. They are always on the fringe of making it. Think of all the people who have gone to Broadway or Hollywood and almost made it. We have "also ran" situations in other areas of life. Frequently people put prayers in the prayer chest, but they manage to obstruct the healing. I have many people who use the prayer chest only from sheer desperation. You know how it goes, "When everything else fails, pray." I truly believe that many healings do not happen because the prayers come into the prayer chest from desperation rather than from a knowingness. Why are some healed and some not? Jesus said that it is done unto you as you believe. You touch the hem of his garment and you are healed. If you scoot around, you are not healed. So let's come from a consciousness, not from desperation. That's a tough one sometimes, but that's what we have to work on.

I like what Dr. Barker says: "More family situations have been healed by keeping hands off the situation than by forcing opinions on the family." I'll drink to that, that's a fantastic statement. We usually think we are correcting a situation by getting our hands into it instead of giving freedom to the situation. You have to be free in a situation to be free of it. You must step back and look at the situation objectively. You can't see the picture if you are in the picture and the picture is in the picture frame. This is why obstruction often keeps us from our healing.

Think about the people who adopt children, the couples who say, "We can't have any children." They go to the doctor and find that there's a physical reason. So they adopt a child. And you know what oftentimes happens. The wife becomes pregnant. How is something like that explained? I know of a couple who wanted children more than anything in the world; they adopted one, and then the wife had twins. So what happened there? To me, the only way that can be explained is that there probably was a subjective obstruction to parenthood. How else can it be explained? In many people there is a subjective fear to parenthood. Adopting a child heals that fear and makes them become aware that they are worthy of being parents. Somewhere along the physical line, something is removed. The obstruction, the clogging, the choking, the impeding, the retarding, is removed, and they have a baby. And oftentimes the obstruction keeps a couple childless.

People frequently say, "I can't have a good job. I never could find the right job. I can never find the right mate." That kind of "I can't" is doing nothing except planting negative thoughts into the subconscious. It is exactly what you don't want. It is a very delicate situation when we put any kinds of thoughts into the subconscious.

I told you a story a couple of years ago about a little girl whose mother was making a dress for her for Christmas. The little girl wanted to wear it right now! And she would ask, "Mommy, when can I wear the dress?" Her mother would answer, "This is for Christmas, honey." Christmas was five months away. How can little children think of what five months means? The calendar means nothing to them. They want their good right now! The little girl could not understand why she had to wait until Christmas. Every time she asked her mother how far away Christmas was, the mother said, "It won't be long now." The child doesn't understand that.

It happened that the mother went to the hospital to have a baby. This delayed the making of the dress, and the little girl could not understand the reason for the delay. And with the bringing in of a baby, she developed the idea that the baby was responsible for her not having the new dress. So you can see how a young mind can gain the belief in obstruction and delay.

What happened is that she developed the feeling of delay. She developed the habit of thinking that all of her good— not only the dress but anything else that she really wanted— had to be waited for and that she would have to go through the torture of waiting. She grew up with a "someday-my-prince-will-come" idea in the Love Department; and with a "someday-my-right-job-will-come" idea in the Job Department.

I wonder how many of us have said: "As soon as the

children grow up, I'll be happy. As soon as the car is paid off, as soon as he gets a good job. As soon as I find my right place, I will be happy." When we say that, it is saying we have a belief in delay.

We don't live in Religious Science with "love is around the corner." Which corner? "Good is around the corner." Which corner? Your good is right here. Let's refer to what Jesus said to his disciples when the harvest was ready. They had said, "No, Master, it is four months till the harvest." Jesus said, "The fields are white to harvest right now."

There's no delay. Because that for which you dream already is in mind. Otherwise, you could never receive it. That for which you pray is already known, it's an accomplished fact—third step of treatment.

Jesus said, "When you pray, believe you have these things." He didn't say, "going to." He didn't say, "will be." He said, "Believe that you have."

You might say, "Well, I don't know. Look at my bankbook. Am I going to look at my zero minus balance and say I already have it?" Treat to know that what you want is already an accomplished fact. *Believe* you have these things.

Let's know that we already have what we need. That which you demonstrate, you are. Emerson said, "Tell me what you talk about all day long with feeling and I'll tell you what you are, what you have, what you believe in."

One of my former teachers said that coronary occlusions often stem from thoughts of obstruction. He said that mental congestion is one of the basic problems of 95 per cent of our illnesses—start congesting the mind and pretty soon the result ends up in the body.

Cause and effect. As you sow, you reap—because Infinite Mind, God, is never blocked. We don't always understand this. But it takes total release when it comes to our prayers. When it comes to why we aren't having our good, if you are giving a single excuse, you are not ready. If you are giving an excuse, your consciousness is not prepared for the harvest. Whenever you give excuses, where is God?

We get tense when things don't go just right. We often hear, "I am going to see that it gets done right!" Of course, "getting it done right" is YOUR way, not God's way. They also say, "I am going to get it done my way OR ELSE." And the "or else" ends up in a heart attack. When people are so built up to pressure and tension and disease, the subconscious says, "Well, I don't know how to get this guy out of this so he's got to have a heart attack."

I know of a case where this man liked this girl very very much and she loved him. But she was cornering him, getting him into the corner to marry her. He just said, "Let's cool it a while." She did not want to accept that, so she put him in a "you-marry-me-or-else-I'll-never-see-you-again" situation. Well, he was confused, he loved her, but he didn't want to get married at this particular time in his life. She went ahead and planned the wedding—the orchestra, the flowers, me, everything, invitations all printed up, and he was forced into a situation he didn't know how to get out of. He had a heart attack. And she wanted to have a bedside ceremony, which really frosted him, you know. But that's the only way he knew, subconsciously, how to get out of that situation. That is not a rare case, but it is an actual case. The point is that the cause and effect are always connected. Sometimes we don't see the cause but we can see the effect.

When you see the effect, can you pinpoint the cause? Can you pinpoint the mental equivalent of that which you are experiencing? Can you pinpoint the cause of your headaches? Can you pinpoint the cause of your ulcers?

Whatever you are congesting in your mind HAS TO come out. An ulcer doesn't occur because you're loving everything in your life. What is the cause for this effect you are experiencing? If you can pinpoint the mental equivalent of that which you believe in, you can understand the effect. We take the aspirin for the headache but not for the cause. What I'm saying is, "Get back to the cause."

Okay, I've painted this picture. It isn't very pretty. But it's some of us. It was once me. What do we do about it? I have spent all this time telling you this little story, but somewhere along the line perhaps I have said something that can key you into knowing that there is an Intelligence within you that is greater than you; that the creation is less than the Creator; that the same intelligence that is guiding the stars is guiding the flow of your body. We get in God's way, don't we? We get in God's way. And as Emerson said, "Get your bloated nothingness out of your way."

Let that Divine hose just flow. Let that Divine hose give you the answers. You don't have to do anything! You have to know the truth about you. But, you see, WE get ourselves into the driver's seat; we think that WE have to do it. It is like we are saying, "Now, God is okay, BUT THIS PROBLEM IS TOO BIG FOR GOD."

Let's get ourselves out of God's way. The moment we do, every prayer is answered at the right time. Geography and calendar have nothing to do with your healing. We don't always realize that the Infinite Knower always knows.

Fear is the darkroom where negatives are developed. So let's come out into the light of our own being. The Infinite Intelligence, God, Divine Being, knows the answer. "The fields are already white with harvest." You might only see the snow, but the potential of spring is right there.

Let's get out of the "I can't" Department into the I CAN. Let's get out of, "It's impossible." Let's not just say, "I'm one with God and I know I'm God and I know I'm a perfect expression of God."

Let us say, "What am I going to do?" As soon as we say that, the answers come.

Let's stay as long as we possibly can with the idea that we do not interfere, by having inner fear. Don't interfere with God's plan, with inner fear. Fears start within. Fears are removed within. So don't interfere with inner fear.

Often we put a prayer in the prayer chest and ask for God's help, but we don't help ourselves. Then we discuss it with our intimate friends who tell us why it's not happening. And we explain all the impossibles: "It's never happened before. I can't. I don't see how. There's no way out." Listen to yourself when you talk like that. How can you expect to be healed if you talk like that?

I say many times to people, "Do you want to be justified or healed? You can't be both. Do you want to be justified about how mistreated you were? How unhappy you are? Do you want to be justified?" If you want to be justified, don't blaspheme. If God isn't answering your prayer, it's not because of God. Don't try to be justified of your injustices, be healed of them.

"Oh, Lord, help mine unbelief." That's the whole story. "Oh, Lord, help mine unbelief."

You might say, while you're sitting there, "He doesn't know what he's talking about." I do. I do, from personal experience and from observation. I do, from observation of what people are doing to themselves—man's inhumanity to man and man's inhumanity to himself. If you walk out of here with a feeling that you're worthy of good and worthy of love and worthy of joy and worthy of God, you won't have a problem. If you walk out the same way you came in, that's all right, you have that freedom. But how long are you going to sit on your principles? Get up and let them work. Everybody should be healed of that which is bothering him. Heal yourself of that which is bothering you.

I simply say in closing, "Get yourself out of God's way." The greatest thing you have is your mind. What are you doing with it? No matter what needs to be done, God can do it.

Don't be justified. Be healed.

Reverend Tom Costa is pastor of the Religious Science Church of the Desert at Palm Desert, California. The church is unique in that every Sunday Reverend Costa gives one service at Palm Desert and later he gives one service at Palm Springs, nearby.

Reverend Costa completed his ministerial training with Dr. Earl Barnum. He began his formal ministerial studies in 1968, commuting more than 25,000 miles in his final 2 years in order to complete his studies. He has been a minister for 6 years.

With a major in psychology and sociology, he graduated from the University of California at Los Angeles in 1955.

Reverend Costa is currently a member of the Board of Directors of RSI.

"Get Out Of God's Way" is a talk Reverend Costa delivered at the Palm Desert Church on April 1, 1979.

CHAPTER SIX

Awareness is a hearing and a seeing from within,
The mind seeing, the mind hearing,
The kind of hearing and seeing that makes for
    wholeness,
For that integrated relationship with ourselves.

—Frantz

Your Relationship with Yourself

By Reverend Joyce Frantz

Your relationship with yourself is the basic, the most important, the most dynamic relationship you can ever have. Oh yes? Why? Because it's the essence, the ingredient we all need to have in order to be really alive.

If we want fulfilling experiences, we need to be able to get along with ourselves. The hardest person to get along with is ourself. If we can get along with ourselves, we'll get along with other people—without question. In this teaching we want more than just to get along—we want to be happy with ourselves. We want to express that happiness so that we are a joy to ourselves and to everyone we meet. That's our objective.

We will have more about that in our lesson today. Right now we want to treat for this time.

First of all, what is a treatment? We say treatment is prayer. Then we add that it's scientific prayer. Sometimes adjectives are superfluous. But in this instance I believe using the word scientific gives us some clarification. According to Webster, the root meaning of scientific is "a marriage." In Latin, "scientia" means "knowledge;" "facere" means "to make." Scientific is to make knowledge. What's more, investigation has proved that the results will always be the correct results based upon knowledge. The knowledge has been tested, and that knowledge has been proved.

What we're really saying is that this is the science of spiritual laws—and by science we mean there is always a cause and there is always an effect. Moreover, we can initiate our own cause. We can initiate our own cause through our words, and we can make the knowledge live. At that point we will be fulfilling one of those 2,000 promises in the Bible, the one that says, "And all things, whatsoever you ask in prayer, believing, you shall receive."

Will you join me in this scientific prayer:

There is one cosmic arena, and I am a cosmic citizen. I am of the whole for the sole purpose for the whole to express through me, as me, to make knowledge come alive. During this hour I will see that this really does happen. I will see *how* it happens. I will see more clearly how I can work with that expression as me, to make knowledge come alive. Then I will be a joy and a delight to myself and to all whom I meet on my pathway, every day, for all time. In this I rejoice. And so be it.

Our lesson this morning is: Your Relationship with Yourself.

You are the greatest and the most important person in your world. How well acquainted are you with the fantastic person you are? Do you really believe you are fantastic? If you really believe it, if you really believe you are fantastic, you truly have a beautiful working relationship with yourself.

However, there may be many individuals who have a

casual relationship or perhaps only a nodding acquaintance with themselves. They may even need an introduction to the real self. They may have never met.

And then there are those individuals who do not like themselves. In fact, they can't stand themselves. Those are the ones who can never be alone. They're always rushing around. They're so busy they have no time for that precious self to ever even nudge them on the shoulder. No time at all. However, they're busy helping everybody else. They are helping all those others whether they want help or not. All this so that they do not ever get to themselves.

Then there are the sick individuals, and some of those have even made a habit of being sick and are chronically ill. Those persons, you know, are so busy expressing their problems in illness that they do not have time to meet the real self. All of their time is taken up with a problem. How could they get to themselves? They're too busy. Besides, they probably do not even suspect the truth about themselves. They may even think and believe a lot of things which aren't true, such as, "Nobody likes me. I'm always the last one. I'll do it when nobody else is around." These untruths may be examples of reasons they do not like themselves.

What is this self we're talking about? Who and what is the real you? There was a time when someone would ask us, "Who are you? What are you?" and our answer was, "I'm Rusty Brown," or "Mary Smith from Gingerville." That's only our name and it's where we live. It doesn't say anything about us. Nothing at all. Yes, those are vital statistics someone put on our birth certificate when we arrived here on this plane. And of course it is valuable information. Let's be glad we have it—because there are places in this land of ours where they only use numbers. But even there, great things can happen. So let's appreciate our name, let's appreciate our body—for what they are.

You and I know our body is the housing, it is that beautiful cathedral, it is the cathedral of the reality of ourselves. And what is the reality? From time to time it has been given so many different names, such as Spirit, Greater Power, Creative Power, First Cause, God, Principle, on and on. But what do those names mean? It's no wonder, with all of those names, that individuals get mixed up.

We are really saying that we are abstract beings and we are endowed with abstract qualities. And that's even more confusing. Are we real or not? And where is all this that we are talking about? Is it in everybody else and somewhere else? And that's really no better than saying that we are Spirit or that we are Greater Power. What words can we use that are descriptive enough so we can really believe and feel what we say?

We can say: Spirit, or God, is in each one of us and It is our life, It is our mind, It is our I Am consciousness. Because It is in us, we know that our life is intelligent. It is— whether we believe it or not.

Can we relate to that? Can we accept that as our family tree, our geneology? Of course we can, because God made everything out of Itself by becoming the thing He made. And that includes every human being, even those who are skeptical.

In truth, God not only created everything—everything that we see—but there is a continuous creating through each person. As it was in the beginning it is always. Creation did not occur just at one time. There is a continuing creativity expressing through every person. And that creativity is initiated through our choices and our selections.

We arrived on this plane as individualizations of the One. We arrived perfect, absolutely perfect. There are no seconds. We are not seconds, and we live with that perfection intact. That is the intelligent life within each one of us—every one of us, everywhere, whether we like it or not. That life is that fantastic you. It is the way we see that intelligent life in us; it is how we feel about it; it is what we do with it; and it is what it does to us, in spite of us, that makes up our relationship with our self.

Why is that relationship with our self so very very important? Why do we say this is the basic, the most dynamic relationship we can ever have? Because it is truly the only relationship there ever is, ever was, is now, or ever will be. It is the only relationship.

The truth is, if we are on good terms with ourselves, we will automatically be on good terms with everyone we meet and with everyone we know. In other words, it's an integrated relationship with ourselves that is the preparation for all living whether at home or on the job. It's the only right kind of preparation for marriage. It's real because it works.

Often, those individuals who have problems with marriage are the ones who want to change the other person. They are never the one who needs changing. It's always the other person. There's nothing wrong with the marriage. It is a great idea. Marriage cannot have problems. It is always people problems. Individuals who come in for counseling ask, "How can I change her?" "How can I change him?" The results are always fabulous when the complainants change. The problem was either no longer there or each one learned how to accept the other person just as they are—because they could see they had expected things that were impossible for that person to give.

We hear comments such as, "He's supposed to make me happy," or "She is supposed to make me happy"—when happiness can only be experienced from within ourselves. It doesn't come to us from out there. It has to bubble over from in here—from within. And when it bubbles over from in here, the other fellow will automatically be happy, because it is contagious. It is catchy. And it's glorious.

We may also hear, "He doesn't love me any more," or "She doesn't love me any more." You and I know the receiving of love is in the loving. When individuals understand that things need to be given instead of received all the time, and that the receiving is in the giving, we will have a much better relationship with ourselves.

There are also those individuals who say, "I will get married and that will solve all my problems, I'll never have another problem to worry about." However, like attracts like. Therefore, many people just create a partnership with their mutual problems. That's not marriage. For instance, a person who can never pay all his bills, who never has enough money at the end of the month or at any time, attracts a person who has an inequity between spending and paying her bills. Why were they attracted to each other? "Oh, there must be chemistry," some people say, "there must be affinity." What is the affinity and what's the chemistry? They wind up with a merger called marriage. Immediately they double the problem. They compound the problem. Two and two always make four. But each person is always blaming the other. "Spendthrift." "He's a spendthrift." "She's a spendthrift." "Can't hold on to money." "Money just flows through her hands." "Money just flows through his hands." On and on.

In any case, we need an integrated relationship with ourselves. It is a fundamental requirement for marriage as well as for every other area of living. And we deserve happiness, we deserve fulfilling experiences, every moment of every day.

What is an integrated relationship with ourselves? "Integrate" comes from the Latin and means "to make whole, to renew." What do we want to make whole or renew? We want to see ourselves as a whole person. We want to live

from that intelligent life within us, that I Am consciousness that is individualized. Great. That means we are of
the Whole, of Spirit, of Spirit which is all Life, Truth, Love,
Being, cause and effect; and It is the only power in the
universe that knows Itself, THAT KNOWS ITSELF. Isn't
that beautiful? That's the power that is within you and
within me.

Awareness, we say, is a hearing and a seeing from within,
the mind seeing, the mind hearing. That's the kind of hearing and seeing that makes for wholeness, for that integrated
relationship with ourselves.

And where does renewal fit in? Renewal makes us like
new, it restores. In my opinion, renewal dates back to the
Garden of Eden, when man's original state was perfection.
Yes, the perfection, the perfection we had before we ate
that apple, or the persimmon, whatever it was. And after
that, after we dined on that fruit, we found out that the life
principle can be used both ways. And maybe we used it
both ways without knowing there were two ways that things
could be done, either good or evil, or freedom or limitation. We just thought that this was the way life is, that this
is it. We may not even have made the distinction. But we
have a choice about which one we want to follow. When we
make the choice and we turn to the Father's house, back
to that perfection, we'll wake up and we'll be like new. We
will be perfect.

And, you know, the son that returned to the Father's
house found no recriminations, no accusations, was received with open arms; the feast is prepared, the table is
always set, everything is there. We're never put out. We just
turn the other way.

That perfection is always within us, but do we always
remember it and believe it? That's why we need to see what
the relationship is with ourselves. Through scientific prayer
we may reveal that perfection bit by bit. But once we have

a healing, the area that has been healed will be permanent. Spiritual healings do not have relapses. That means you and I do not have relapses in that area. *When there's a real healing one can never return to former modes of living.* Never. Isn't that great? Isn't that wonderful? Once we're aware it is ours, oh, that harvesting—that's where we rejoice in bringing in the fruit of the harvest. When we have this I Am consciousness awakened, that's when we are aware of it. When we are aware of it, we can have the phenomenal changes in our lives.

Why are changes possible? From this vantage point we'll be seeing everything from this I Am consciousness. We will no longer be living out there in the material world, we will be living in here, from within. We will be living from our endowment, our heritage, from the light that's within us. It won't be the environment, it won't be people, it won't be "things" that are important. We would be breaking the First Commandment to put all of that before God. You know, "Thou shalt have no other gods before me." There are many things we will change. We will no longer be doing it the way our father or mother did it. "Why not? If it was good enough for them, isn't it good enough for me?" No, it isn't. What was good enough for your father is *not* good enough for you. What was good enough for your mother is *not* good enough for you. If we haven't learned more than they learned, we've been standing still. If you, as students, don't learn more than I, as a teacher, have learned, something is amiss.

So let's go on, let's care, let's change, because each one of us is a unique individualization of That I Am—with our beautiful dowry—who is the Knower and the Doer, the Knower and the Doer that is within us. And It never repeats Itself. We are the only repeaters. We don't have to have the same thing twice.

Who has oatmeal every morning? Who has cereal every

morning? Why? Why do you have the same cereal every day? Why do you get out of the same side of the bed every day? There are four sides to it, or three anyhow, that are very accessible. So aren't we creatures of habit? And why? We're sclerotic in our thinking. Our thinking hardens up and doesn't give us any room. We realize with this I Am that there doesn't need to be the same old stuff. We never liked corned beef hash seven days a week. We want new things every day. And there is a way that is just right for you, just right for me, and it's not the same for Johnnie or Jack or Mabel or Mary. It is just right for us because we are unique. Each one of us is a unique individualization, and there will be something new, and it will be just for us.

Whenever we turn to this I Am That I Am, this is our connection with that cosmic encyclopedia. That I Am in you *is* that cosmic encyclopedia. It's for you to use. It's for me to use. Surely we need to take the initiative, we need to start the action. We can't just sit and rock and expect the world to be landing at our feet. No. We have to move into action and make the knowledge live. All this comes to us through our awareness, through the ideas that we get. All of us get ideas. Remember, Rawson states that 200 ideas flow through our consciousness every minute. Certainly there must be some there that look good to you, some that are just ripe for the picking, some that we need to choose and give life to, in order that this knowledge may live through us. Let's pick them. Let's select them. You can be particular, because there are that many. There's the great abundance. All this from awareness, from within ourselves.

We could not really wear someone else's experience. It would not fit us. It would not feel good. It would not be comfortable. The shoes might not always fit us. But in addition to that, we do not need to settle for seconds. We don't need to settle for second-hand experiences either. First-hand is what we want to have, because we are entitled to it. We deserve to have first-hand experiences, because you can hew out of life all of those fabulous new experiences that you deserve, that I deserve—not the warmed over and used up ones that have all the edges nibbled away by somebody else.

Let's begin now by relating to ourselves. "Relate" comes from a Latin word meaning "to refer." "Refer" means "to carry back," back to the I Am consciousness. It always goes back to the one thing—to the Father within, to the I Am consciousness, to this one Infinite Universal Whole of which we are, and the precious beautiful self we are. It is where we experience life, and we experience it from within ourselves, not out there. The experiences of life aren't out there whether we play or work or whatever we're doing. It is really in our consciousness that our living takes place. That's where we can make knowledge live. We can do that because we're no longer in bondage to yesterday. Nor do we let tomorrow steal today away from this fabulous living that we're doing right now.

Oh, yes, we will be working first-hand from this I Am consciousness. We will *live* this wonderful self as we were intended to. And there are no limits on it. The infinite potential is unlimited, and that is available to each one of us through this I Am consciousness that each one of you is. I Am. You are. We have this wonderful self because we know who and what we are. And we're no longer in bondage to ill-founded ideas or to false gods, where money or the material good are more important than our integrated relationships.

We can do our choosing and selecting with wisdom because we will be guided from within ourselves, not because somebody approves of what we're doing, and not because somebody says, "Yes, you do it first." We will be guided from within because we have approval from within ourselves. And we know when we hear truth that it rings a bell in us. We know that nobody can say, "That's right," when we feel honestly in our heart and soul that it is not right. We can always tell.

If we could only remember, if we always live from the I Am, from that indwelling kingdom, all other things will be added unto us. It is another promise.

Money is beautiful, of course it is. You know that beautiful green stuff with all those faces of presidents and everything, beautiful stuff. But it is effect. It's not cause to anything. Money cannot bring us spiritual rewards. It can bring us a soft bed. But do you know that soft beds can sometimes become so hard that we may not be able to sleep on them? So what's wrong? It's like we're sleeping on the money. Does money make a good bed? Maybe not that good. You've heard about those individuals who are found dead, who starved to death with money for their pillow—it didn't do them any good. We know that money doesn't buy answers or happiness. We also know that every year statistics show there are always some millionaires who commit suicide. So it is not money alone. And isn't it surprising? You wouldn't believe that people who had all the money to do all the things they might want to do would commit suicide. And we say, "Weren't they silly? What I could have done with that million!" Not if you were in the same place that they were, not if you were sitting on the same pile of problems they were sitting on. They were so uncomfortable that life was intolerable to them. So they committed suicide. All because they had put the cart before the horse. The cart is full of money. Yes, it's even overflowing with money, but the horse is not there to pull it away, to keep it in circulation. And hoarded money can serve no man, not even the person who is piling it up.

Okay, in the relationship with ourselves we love the self

that we are, that "wonderful me" that each one of us is. That means that we accept ourselves. We accept ourselves exactly the way we are.

If there are things we do not like—perhaps we have some hurt feelings piled up over here; and in another corner we may have a little resentment; we may have some hostility; and we may have some other kind of negative. We, of course, are accepting ourselves, so we do not hurt the things that we do not like. We will not react or fight them, because we know how to fix those unwelcome intruders, and we'll be free of them. *But that doesn't mean because we have them we are going to say, "I'm no good," or all of these other kinds of things that are devastating to us.*

In the I Am consciousness, we have the capacity to choose what we want. We also have the power, which acts as a law, to change those unacceptables. That is the super, super life that we rejoice in. The Knower and the Doer is right here within us. It isn't out there. It isn't on that job. It isn't in that girl, in that man. It is within us: the Knower and the Doer.

There may be times when things we have done are not too intelligent. Even if they don't check out it's only an indication of where we are. It's not an indication of right or wrong. Why should we condemn ourselves? Why should we put ourselves down? We punish ourselves for something we did because that's where we were at the time we did it. Why should we place ourselves outside of the serenity and the peace of the home which is established within ourselves— this I Am consciousness that we really are? We don't need to punish ourselves. Worst of all, why hijack ourselves out of our self-respect so that our self-esteem gets shattered in pieces, so much so that it is almost impossible to get us put back together? *Almost* impossible.

Thank God that *nothing* is impossible to this Infinite Oneness; we become aware that there is a place we can turn to, to have all things renewed and restored. After all, it was our creation, this thing that we did, and it did not just happen. We used a lot of energy to do it. We used a lot of energy to do it in the first place, even if it was unintelligent. We will use our wisdom to transform that creation, instead of reacting and being frustrated and beating ourselves.

This relationship with ourselves is like a marriage. We cannot take anything for granted. Every idea that we want to experience will be meticulously selected. Is that what happens in marriages? I wonder. That's what should happen in marriages. Marriages between individuals should not be taken for granted. But you know pretty much what happens after that glow from the honeymoon. Do we try to be the individuals that we were before we went on the honeymoon? We take each other for granted. Within ourselves we cannot take ourselves for granted. We cannot know that things will just be. If we don't choose, if we don't select, we'll have an average kind of life that doesn't really go anywhere.

We can choose the heights. We are entitled to the heights because we are individualizations. We're special, every one special and unique, so we will select. Every experience will be selected thoughtfully, meticulously. They will be checked out with that Intelligence within us and we will have a right feeling about it. We won't be squirmy or squeamish about it. We will know it is right. Then we will know that we are guided intuitively for integrated action. Yes, we'll be mind-seeing, mind-hearing, as awareness. And then we'll see knowledge live in our experience. And, you know, all of us can do this every day. We are expected to do it.

I had an experience this week I would like to share with you. Do you recall last Sunday I talked about the executive committee of the board of trustees signing a contract for your minister to be on radio beginning April 3rd? I reported to you that the representatives from the station said the script as submitted was low key. And, of course, you know usually low key is supposed to be a compliment. But low key in this instance wasn't a compliment. As a matter of fact, it was unsatisfactory. It was a reject. So I was to be at WHLI on Friday at 11 a.m. Several times during the week I picked up that folder and rewrote the script. Finally, on Friday morning somehow it occurred to me. From where? From that Intelligence within me came the awareness. I was trying to do an hour's teaching in one minute. That was really to be God's commercial. So now it all cleared.

I sat down on Friday morning at 10 a.m. and wrote up those two commercials within ten minutes. I submitted them at 11 a.m. at WHLI. Their comment was, "That is the commercial! We'll use it exactly the way it is!" That's Intelligence beaming through. That's the happening. That's the knowledge, the way to make knowledge live. But we have to have mind-hearing, we have to have mind-seeing, from that Intelligence within us. And when it's right there, it's right everywhere.

How to make knowledge live. Isn't it wonderful? You can do that, I can do that. But then the other sideline is that when I arrived at the station on Friday, the individual who greeted me had a long face and said, "**I** really ought to come and see you privately because I went to the dentist and he gave me a horrible toothache." And I said, "What were you doing while he gave you the toothache?" And he said, "Who me?" And with that we were interrupted and went into the conference which had started at that point. So we did the recording, and everything went in the right order. And as we were walking to the elevator, he said, "Say, what did you do? I no longer have a toothache."

So with these kinds of things that happen all the time, knowledge lives from within. And it's the same kind of experience that I think I shared with you that I had when we were buying the house that's now the parsonage. Several times I needed to see the real estate lady in connection with buying the house. I sat beside her desk this one day, and as we were busily talking I became consciously aware that people were brushing past me. They were touching me. Finally after t⸍ ⸍ourth or the fifth one I looked up, and the g⸍⸍ ⸍⸍one all the transactions with us said, "Do ⸍⸍at they want to touch you because ever since . ⸍⸍with Religious Science of Long Island, I've b⸍ ⸍s right and left? They haven't been selling ⸍ ⸍nt some!"

So it's ⸍ ⸍ know—how do you make knowledge live⸍ ⸍l when we live from in here? We live from ⸍ ⸍t. In any case, every experience can be a joy ⸍ ⸍ur soul, yes, when we love.

After all, . ⸍ ⸍essence—it's the ingredient of the relationsh⸍ ⸍ which is truly the only relationship there .

Reverend Frantz is ⸍ ⸍Religious Science Church of Long Island, New Yo⸍ ⸍lk, "Your Relationship with Yourself," there on Mar⸍

Erratum: para. 5, line 1, should read: "this is back teacher we had—in the early 1880s—" Page 26, para. 5, line 1

CHAPTER SEVEN

The energy of the universe is thought. That which holds us together and keeps us in harmony and balance, health and order is thought.

—Graves

The Rationale of Treatment

Dr. Roy Graves

Someone once said that man becomes what he thinks about all day long. We could complain bitterly about weather and conditions and taxes and prices and Christmas—God knows what else. But it doesn't solve the situation at all, does it? It puts us in a condition of being restless, unhappy, cantankerous, irritable; and if we persist in that kind of thought, eventually, of course, it has a profound effect on our bodies and an effect on our relationships. Obviously, that's the beginning of the corruption of our whole system of work.

I believe that we can handle the things that come to us, for we have been given dominion over the things of the earth. Now, if we have been given dominion, by what means have we been given dominion? What is greater than the things of the earth? It is a man's thought. A man's thought —this is the thing, this is the one element, that has dominion over the things of the earth. And yet, look at what we do with our capacity to think, to reason, our power to know. My thoughts today are going to run in that direction.

How much thought do we have? How much freedom do we have to work our thoughts for better or for worse? And how can we learn how to use our thoughts for a constructive, positive, affirmative togetherness—not only in our own lives but in our community?

If I were to tell you about a tree, a marvelous maple tree that grew on our front lawn back home—now, you have never seen the tree, it doesn't mean anything to you—you will walk out of here today and not even think about that tree. And yet every time I think of home I think of that maple tree that we used to hang rubber tires on to swing on. We used to climb up into the maple tree to hide. No one ever found us there, and if they found us they couldn't get at us. That maple tree was a major part of my life. It doesn't mean anything to you. You never saw it.

Unless we know a thing, it doesn't have anything to do with us. This, I think, is the reason why the impact of an understanding of God has had such a tremendous effect on our lives, because suddenly we are able to understand God in terms that make a difference to us, that come right down to where we live, that change the very feel of our skins. By what? By some process of understanding, by some process of knowledge. So it is what we *know* that changes our lives, and it is what we *know* that allows us to ruin our lives, or to paddle along by concensus. It is what we *know* that makes the difference.

Someone once said to me, "I don't know why I bother to go to listen to you." He came back a couple of times and he began to listen, and it was sometime afterward that he said, "I need to know what the spiritual premise is on which you base what you call your healthy-mindedness." I say, "Yes, it's based on a *spiritual* premise."

I want to set out that spiritual premise, because everybody is afraid to be talked to about God, about Spirit. And I am going to appeal to your sense of logic. I am going to see if we can roll this thing out in a very easy and simple way that does not offend anyone's theology but returns it to a place where we can put it in our minds and know that we have it with us.

First of all, I think we must distinguish between Jesus, God, and Christ—because this is the premise on which we base our reasoning. I don't want to go into too much depth, but for those of you who have never heard me say it before, I want to say that God is Life. It is that Life that has made everything out of Itself; and that Life, in order to be eternal, must, obviously, in and of Itself, be self-existent. That means it has everything that is necessary for its own perpetuity.

Life never had a beginning and never had an end. You see, we so often equate life with "my human experience." No, I'm asking you to think about that Eternal Life, Life Itself. That maple tree is going to live long after I'm dead, I hope. There are kids still hiding in it, wearing its bark smooth with their little sneakers, going up and down the trunk—as they must and should. There's life in that tree, there's life in me, there's life in you. The scientists say there's life in this lectern, a molecular, atomic, electrical energy here. There is life, one life, universal—and that life is God. It must, in and of Itself, have all intelligence, all reason, all power. And there must be no flaw in It or It would have destroyed Itself. You don't mind my saying "Itself" rather than "Himself;" we need to depersonalize it within ourselves. God, then, is that universal life force. All right? I'm using synonyms here, I'm not changing my direction, I'm trying to find some word that will appeal in the broadest sense. It is that life force that has given birth to us. It is that force, and not we ourselves, which has made us. We are the sheep of its pasture. And when it calls we respond. That's life.

Now, Jesus was a human being, a man not unlike you and me. Two legs, two arms, and a head. And he walked on the earth. Now, did he go to India? I don't know. Did he sit with the Tibetan monks? I don't know. Did he go to London and help to build the London Bridge? I don't know. I've heard all kinds of theories, and I don't know. I wasn't there. But one thing I do know—that this man knew the kind of God that I'm defining today. He said that God is Spirit and that those who would worship It must worship It in spirit. And what is spirit but knowledge and understanding?

Jesus knew his God. He was not the only one to know his God. Moses knew his God. Buddha knew his God. And a lot of you know your God. In fact, Jesus knew his God so well that we gave him a title, and that title that we gave him was, "The Christ," which literally means, "The Annointed, the Enlightened One." Back in those days we gave those kinds of titles to people. Now we give titles such as "Reverend" and "Doctor" and "Psychiatrist." But they gave Jesus the title, "The Christ." Who gave him that title? Who was the one who was able to measure that kind of erudition? The "Christ" is a Greek word, it wasn't even put on by his disciples. They recognized with such clarity his teachings about God that they didn't have to put a name on him; it was enough that they revered him as one of their brothers. So the Greeks put the word "Christ" on the man, Jesus, whose name was not Jesus anyway. It was probably Emmanuel.

In the beginning God, before which there was nothing and after which there is nothing but the expressions of Itself, unfolding by means of man, by humankind, and by all forms of life; and everything is alive with a natural, inherent life force, including Jesus and you and me and the Buddha; and we call ourselves Mr., Mrs., Miss, Ms., Doctor, Reverend, Pope, Chief—whatever. We put on labels to identify ourselves, or we allow others to label us. So, let's get clear then, when we are talking about God we are not talking about Jesus, and when we are talking about Christ we are not talking about Jesus. "Christ" was not his last name. He was Jesus, and he probably existed.

I am much more interested in the teachings *of* Jesus than I am in the teachings *about* Jesus. Why? Because he taught that Christ-Consciousness which is in you and me.

How can I hope to have that mind in me that was in Christ Jesus unless it be universal, unless it be one mind that we can all share? Are we talking about brain? No. We're talking about mind, we're talking about a sense of values, a sense of rightness, a sense of intelligence, a knowledge of God.

Let that knowledge of God be in you that was in Jesus. Simple? It is so simple and so beautiful, I wonder why we have not all caught it from our first days of self-consciousness—except that we get talked out of it, I expect. "We are not worthy, we are sinners, we are condemned, we are born in the flesh, we suffer in the flesh, we die in the flesh." I was not born in the flesh, I was born of love. I was born with that Christ-Consciousness, I was born out of that reality of the Presence of God, just as you were. We are born in love, we are not born in sin. And it's love that keeps us alive, not sin.

You see, then, that there is a divine ideal, there is a divine norm, as Thomas Troward calls it. The divine norm, then, is that Christ Mind, or the knowledge of God. The sense of values, the sense of integrity, the sense of discretion, honesty, self-appreciation, affection for each other—this is what it is to know God. It is not to sit in a dark cave somewhere. No. It is to appropriate one's own inherent gifts, one's own talents, one's own rightness, one's own propriety. This divine ideal then, of course, is the purpose of all religious teaching in every community, to teach this divine norm that all men aspire to. If it be a spiritual teaching, that's all it can teach, and more it need not teach. Nothing else can be taught, nothing else needs to be taught—except *that Christ Mind,* which is the knowledge of God that inherently resides in all of us, but about which we need to be made more aware, and constantly.

Someone has said, "The world is too much with us." We stumble and bump into things all week long and we wonder, "How shall there be any salvation?" So we provide time and space and quiet to come together to take another look at these spiritual values, to come together to look at the business of this divine norm, the understanding of God. "What is good about me? What is right about me?" The most right about us is that we are in control of our own faculties and that we can develop and evolve and promote this inner awareness of the goodness and the rightness of ourselves. Not because we are selfish, not because we are egotistical, but because we are, according to the claim, "sons and daughters of the Most High." We have inherited the qualities of God. If God is the life force, from where else can we get our life? What else can give life except God Itself? God is Life. And if we have God's life within us we must necessarily incorporate the qualities of God. So what God is, I am.

Jesus said, "My Father and I are one." What a beautiful statement! What I have to do then is to be consciously aware of it. I need to sit down, I need to think about it, I need to be aware that I have to practice it. I need to live as though it were so. I need to rejoice and enjoy it. The love of God— which is really the enjoyment of God—is the most freeing force in the world, for then you know that you are in love with that which is eternally good and right and strong and intelligent and joy-giving.

You know, we are not long-faced in Religious Science. We live a life according to what we believe, and that's why we stand tall and confident. We know that we have inherited the gifts of God.

One of our teachers said, "The saddest people in the world are those who are half into mind and half out of matter." Today we would say they are neither fish nor fowl. We would urge them to fish or cut bait. Right? "Half into mind and half out of matter." They know what they ought to do, and they can't quite bring themselves to do it. Or, they know what they ought not do, and they're half-way doing it. Those are the sad people. They have not committed themselves to fish or fowl, to flesh or God. That's a very difficult position to be in.

I'm proposing today, then, that we take an hour to look at Mind and look away from matter and see how much gratification, how much fulfillment, we can achieve in this spiritual understanding. Does it strengthen our minds and our hearts? Does it strengthen our life and our society? I happen to think so, and I'll tell you why. When we know that we're devoted to a higher cause than just ourselves, we tend to do more than just we ourselves could do. It's called enthusiasm, commitment. Right? Enthusiasm literally means "en" meaning "in," and "Theos" means "God." We are "in God," to be enthusiastic. The people who are in God and who are in love with God are enthusiastic about life. Young people talk about turning on to life. Exactly. Because we're so vitally alive, we want to do something intelligent, something constructive; we want to make our world a little better than the way we found it. And I am not going to presume how you must do that.

Today I want us to talk a little bit about "How shall we reshape our minds?"—so that we can make some kind of a viable contribution to ourselves and to our world.

There are three categories, perhaps, of prayer. It might help to define these three so that you know what I'm talking about.

There is prayer which is supplication to an outside God, begging and pleading with God to do this, that, or the other thing for us—making a deal with an outside power. "I'll do this if you do that." That's prayer. I don't believe in that— and I'll tell you why—because I don't believe that appealing to an outside power is nearly as effective as appealing to an inside power. Appealing to an inside power turns us on. Appealing to an outside power can often turn us off. We think of God as a person with human ears and human emotions and human reaction. I can't believe in that God any more.

I believe that God is life, and I think our highest prayers are those delivered to ourselves. And that's called meditation. Sitting in the quiet of your own soul and thinking things through and sorting through your own life and coming to terms about yourself and about your world and the things you like and the things you don't like—meditation has a very quieting effect.

Oftentimes people use meditation as a preparation for treatment, which is the third form of prayer. Treatment is giving direction, specific and intelligent purpose to one's self. It is affirming and appropriating those inherent gifts which were ours from the beginning, which we may have long since lost sight of and sometimes even denied. The greatest sin in the world, Emerson says, is ignorance. Therefore, treatment is the highest form of intelligence, where we are talking to ourselves about that which is true. Not just opinion, not just impression, not just vague hope, not preference, but that which is true. We can't improve on that.

How can I tell you what is true? I ask you to look around. What is truly true? What is *so*? What is reality? Oh, I know, we like to appropriate our own little kind of reality. But, if you really want to straighten out your life, if you really want to get ahead, if you really want to establish your own strength and identity, then it seems to me the most powerful thing we can do is to determine what is true, what is real, what is eternal. You see, the truth is infinite. It is not kept in any corner, it is not possessed privately by any person, it doesn't belong to any teaching. That which is true *is* true. In spite of all the lies that have been said about it, the truth is still the truth. Treatment is the discussing with ourselves, for a specific purpose, what the truth is.

I believe the truth is, first of all, that there is only one God. All men worship It and call It by different names. And that one God, out of which everything has been made —if you need Scriptural Text read the first chapter, the first verse of John—therefore must be more than just a human person. So, it must be where I am and it might even be what I am. And if it is the life force and there is life in me, then there is some chance that I might be able to re-direct my own life. Therefore, I now declare that I have the intelligence of God, in spite of grades and marks and I.Q. and all the rest of the nonsense that people have laid on me. I now declare my independence and my freedom from any wrong opinion about myself.

And since God so loved the world that He gave birth to it, I must also have love. I must be love and, therefore, I am loving; therefore, I am loved. I am loved by the Infinite. I'm loved by the whole world. And I now determine that from this day forward and forever more I shall act as though it were so. I shall act as though the world loves me because I love *it*. I love it because it first loved me. The world and I are one. I want love in my life, and I know that as I project love it bounces back to me, because my world is nothing but a mirror of my own consciousness, what I believe about myself. I look out upon my world. And do you know what? I will call it very good. I will call it very good, and it will tend to become good, because of my view of it and the projection of my life force into it.

I also acknowledge that that perfect health, that perfect orderly balance—mental, physical, emotional and spiritual health—is mine. God did not invent life to be corrupted and to be distorted and to be weakened and to be compromised, but God created life that it should have its fulness. Therefore, I am full of the health of God. And if I understand anything about the creative process, I must assume, by observation if by no other means—I look out upon my world and I say to myself, "You weren't here a thousand years ago and this lecture hall wasn't here a thousand years ago and this tree wasn't here a thousand years ago; they must have come about through some kind of—what can I call it?—something was happening, some creative process. Ah, creative process! God must be all creativity then. Since there is nothing else, I must have within me a capacity to create and to recreate and to renew and to refresh. Oh, yes, that's what I do with my body; I heal my body; I heal my thoughts. It's a creative process taking place in me. I see what it is. I no longer have to appeal to an outside God, nor live in fear thereof. I don't have to worry about God dropping thunderbolts on me now. I understand that God and I are one and that I can appropriate the gifts of God, the qualities of God. I can become God to my own world."

I wonder if that's what Jesus meant when he said, "When we become one with the law we are above the law." I guess I'd better think that through. What in the world does he mean? Now, can I offend the law and still win? No. What he meant is: When we understand how the law works, the understanding of God, then the law works for us and we are no longer opposed to it. The officer stops us on the street and he says, "You were doing 56 miles an hour." "Oh, officer, I'm sorry," I say, "I didn't see the sign that said 55 miles an hour." And he says, "That's your problem, not mine." You can say to God, "I'm sorry, I did not understand that I could not send out hate and get love back." And God will say, "That's your problem, not mine." Ignorance of the law is what? No excuse.

So it seems that we must learn the laws of life, basic, pure, and simple. And that, of course, is the whole spiritual life. That is the spiritual experience. The knowledge of the law— not between good and bad. For we recognize there is no bad except that which has come to pass; and since it's on its way out, I'm not going to give it any time. My mind is now focused on that which is yet to be. The spiritual plums are there for the plucking and have been from the beginning of time. "I and my Father are one" is perhaps the greatest revelation in the whole process of spiritual unfolding. "I am what thou art, thou art what I am."

Moses went up out of Egypt and took his brothers and sisters in spirit to the gates of the Holy Land. And what did he tell them? "I Am That I Am." Marvelous discovery. "Whatever the universe is, I Am; I Am whatever it is. What truly is, I Am." Wonderful teaching.

I'm sure glad that he cleaned it up and brought it up to date and presented it again, but it wasn't new with Moses. Moses grew up in Egypt, remember, in the palace of the Pharaoh, and on the stone lintel over the temple were carved the magic words "Nuk Pu Nuk"—"I Am That I Am." Ancient understanding was that there was only one God and that one God stood back of all life. Our wisest use of prayer is to understand that, to use it, and to remind ourselves of it.

God is not standing at a distance in judgment. God is our ever present help in every need, by means of our new understanding. We can change our thoughts, we can change our direction can't we? You know that. You do it all the time. Is it too much of a leap in faith to say that we can also change our lives? For where our minds go our lives follow right after. Your body will get up out of your seat and go out through those doors and go back on home, and you'll go to brunch and have a beautiful afternoon in the nice crispy sunshine.

Do you get my point? Your body is going to do exactly what your mind tells it to do. Not any more and not any less.

We can bring ourselves to a point of self-realization. To do that in the most glorified way is to recognize that God has given us the freedom to recognize Itself in us. The true self-recognition is the recognition of God. And the recognition of God is the true self-recognition. Not selfishness; it is ultimate selflessness. We recognize that when we abandon our little selves we become part of a cosmic self, and then this little self begins to take on greater meaning, greater purpose, and greater destiny.

Let me answer an unspoken question, "Why then does treatment not work? If this prayer is one of self-appropriation, why does it not work?" May I say that it always works? Your doubt causes doubt to work. Your fear causes fear to work. And if your treatment is full of fear you get nothing but more fear. For your soul doth magnify according to the law. "My soul doth magnify the Lord." My soul doth magnify according to the law. Therefore, I put into my soul that expansive quality of my life—those things that we want.

Treatment works. It works even when it appears not to be working. If your treatment does not work, take a look at what went into it. Did you treat in panic? Was your treatment guilt-ridden? Was your treatment one of fear? Or did you appropriate those gifts of serenity, of security, of self-discipline, self-esteem and of self-appreciation? Treat on the positive side of the ledger and you'll find that that's what develops.

So then we have these three. We can appeal to a non-existent to do the impossible. We can appeal to others to think and to do for us so that we may stand approved in their sight, and somehow muddle through. Or we may stand approved of God, take up the threads of our own lives and leave this world better than we found it. The choice is ours. And as Joshua said in the Old Testament, "As for me and my household, we shall worship the law."

Dr. Roy Graves is currently the pastor of the Winter Park Church of Religious Science in Florida. He has been a minister in Religious Science for 13 years, and his previous Religious Science church affiliations were in New York City and Chicago. His ministerial training was with Dr. Raymond C. Barker, Dr. Claudine Whitaker, and Dr. Docia Norris. Dr. Graves' talk, "The Rationale of Treatment," was presented at the Winter Park church on December 10, 1978.

In addition to his duties as pastor, Dr. Graves has traveled extensively throughout the United States presenting lectures to diverse groups. In those talks, he gives lively and clear explanations of the teachings and ideas of Religious Science.

At an early age, Roy Graves had a natural interest in religion. He was born into a devout Christian family in New England but eventually found himself questioning some of the tenets of traditional churches. His interest in religion caused him to look into the various approaches to it and, in time, to study for the ministry.

Dr. Graves is a past member of the Board of Directors of Religious Science International and is also the District President of the Florida International New Thought Alliance.

CHAPTER EIGHT

It's not where we start that really matters,
It's what we do along the way.

—Grayson

Strategy for a New Life

Dr. Stuart Grayson

For the benefit of our radio audience, this is Stuart Grayson speaking. I am minister of this church, the First Church of Religious Science, speaking from Alice Tully Hall here in Lincoln Center.

Religious Science offers us something quite special. It offers us the ability to consciously change our lives. I don't know anyone who doesn't want to change. I know many people who refuse to do much about it, but I don't know many who don't really want a change in their lives. And so I would like to quote a very brief statement from Arnold Toynbee, who wrote this in his book on civilization, and it applies exactly to what we do here. This is a quote that was actually a theme of a seminar I gave last spring. He said, "You are a voyage, not a harbor," meaning that you are a movement, an action, not a condition, not something settled. And this is what we need to realize—that we are all in process, that we are always moving, that we are always growing, that the question is always coming to us: Which way? Which way? Where is your vision? Where is your outlook?

83

Our study of Religious Science gives us a philosophy, a methodology, that is scientific because it is based on law that is provable, law that we can experiment with and see presented before us as a tangible action in its fruits. It gives us a point of view that allows us to work with ourselves in a marvelous way. And so our Religious Science is not only a religion for many of us, but it is, as well, a way of life, a science of life, a means of producing the most wonderful experiences of fulfillment and satisfaction and joy. We realize there is a price, and we know there is nothing that is absolutely free. The gift of change, the gift for change, the gift to work on ourselves, is there, certainly. But what we do with it is the price we pay. The energy we put forth is the price.

"Are you willing to put forth energy?" says Religious Science to us. "Are you willing to really work on yourself? Do you really want to see that you are literally a voyage?—that you are not just set?—that you are not a harbor sitting there? If you realize that you are that voyage, do you want to work with the trip? Do you want to make it a marvelous, new experience? You can!" That's what it is telling us.

And so our whole work is for the purpose of realizing—no matter what our age is; no matter what our condition is; no matter who we are, what we are or where we are—that there is a possibility, here and now, for change for the better.

I have a news report for you, and that is that Dr. Barker is probably having his greatest successes on the west coast now. He has been giving some seminars, and I understand that the attendance is simply enormous. So he's been very happy in that his work is growing and expanding. It has always been in the world and in this country, but now he's able to go out and bring the great Truth to many other people, as he understands it and as he sees it.

Well, your ministers do move about the world. On Wednesday I flew to Central America. I was there for one day on Thursday and flew back on Friday so that I could be rested here for today. A year ago, in the torrid zone of Central America, I saw a man who was in the midst of complete desolation. He was physically ill, he was mentally and emotionally distressed. He was in a business crisis. I would say that almost every area of his life was in some kind of turmoil.

I had taken several Science of Mind textbooks down there with me and gave him one. In our conversation, I said, "Look, I can't stay here very long, and I can't tell you very much, but I can promise that if you will work with this book and slowly read it and reread it, you will get help. I will give you all the help I can while I am here, and I agree that it is not too much, but the book is here. The textbook for you is in your hand. It is now up to you to see if you will change your life and if you will change your experience."

When I went back there, I found the following. He is in a new office that is absolutely beautiful. He had people waiting there just to shake my hand, just to meet me.

He said, "I want to tell you something. I have had a 360-degree change in my life." What he really meant was that he had had a total revolution and a total change. He said, "I am not the same person, I don't feel the same."

I said, "I know you don't *look* the same," because he looked wonderful.

He said, "My family relationships are different. My business certainly has prospered tremendously and is different. My whole world has been revolutionized. I spend twenty minutes every day reading this textbook, studying it. Then I have my quiet meditation time, and I do my spiritual treatment as best I can." Then he asked, "When are you coming to teach?"

I answered, "Well, you will now be the committee chairman, and you can set up a little seminar, and a group of us will come down one day."

But the marvelous thing is to see what can happen to people who are really starved for change, who are really searching for something new in their lives. That was a great experience for me, that meeting in Costa Rica.

"Strategy For A New Life"—what a wonderful promise that holds! And it is possible. And we can have it. And I trust that by the time that we are through with our lesson this morning, we will have some direction as to the way to work on that strategy.

I think the first thing that we need to realize is that there is nothing foreordained in life or about life. For many people, this is exceedingly difficult to accept; and for some people, it is almost impossible to understand. This is because there are a good number of religions that actually teach that one is foreordained to a particular circumstance or condition. That appears in the Judeo-Christian tradition and in the religions of the world. They teach that man has certain qualities that he's born with; that man has certain conditions that have been given to him and that these are in some way an action of a God or an action of the primal cause and that one can't do too much about it; and that one has to simply cooperate and live and pray with continuity of deep prayer and appeal to life, to God, to perhaps give some help.

We know that we have nothing foreordained about us except that there is an infinite good—evolving, unfolding, progressive, onward, forward, moving good. It is the evolutionary process in the universe. So, in that sense, I suppose we are foreordained to good, to harmony, and to unfolding greatness of being that are parts of the progressive movement of life; and it depends upon us as to whether we are going to understand this, to accept it, to work with it, or to just drift along with life's often difficult and sometimes apparently meaningless activities and actions.

If we are not foreordained to anything but good, and if our lives seem to be a mixture of good and medium and of some things not so very good, where is the balance of power? Where is that action or that element that works through us that can help us move in that direction—not of just the medium or the not so good or maybe the occasional very good—of action that can work with the evolutionary process with a forward movement, with the great good that is? Where is that balance of power? It's in your mind.

But it is not only in your mind. It is in your emotions. It is not only in your emotions. It is in your thought and feeling in combination. And so we begin to see that there is something called "belief" operating in us. So we are foreordained to that which operates according to our belief.

Many of us who study the Science of Mind—which is this scientific process with the religious science, religious, philosophical, spiritual, system—accept this on the surface. We say, "Well, we've studied the Science of Mind, and we know there is a science of the mind, and we realize that everything is in our thought and in our feeling and that there is a belief structure that we have and that it operates as a law; therefore, we had better watch our beliefs."

I don't think that we can understand strongly enough that our belief is related to where our vision is; that our belief is related to our attitude toward life and toward ourselves; that our belief is related to the way we act and react within the conditions of the world; and that we need to be constantly watchful about our thoughts and feelings and attitudes, through observing our actions and our reactions. When you observe your actions and your reactions, you see who and what you really are.

I know many people and I have many students who are excellent as far as their knowledge of the Science of Mind is concerned. But when they call me on the telephone to cry out, as it were, "Oh, look what *happened,*" I see that their reaction is not at the level of what they talk about and what they seem to have learned. Their reaction is really at the level of their belief, and their belief is operating as a law in their lives, and this law is really not a law of the great science of being. It is, instead, the law of the world's opinion and the world's beliefs and of the circumstances and conditions and of everything that has happened "out there." They have recognized that change comes through spiritual knowing, that change comes through what we call scientific prayer, that change comes when we get an inreach to the deeper sense of mind. Yet, with their belief structures, with their operation in life, they reveal that their understanding, that their point of view, is superficial, it's academic, it has nothing to do with the deep, innermost part of their being. If it did, they would not cry out so quickly. Surely they would state the fact, "This has happened, this is wrong, this took place." Certainly we face facts. There is nothing about the Science of Mind that tells you that you must not face the facts of life—the physical, material life and existence you have. But, it does tell you, "Face the facts; look through the facts; see something that is more than the facts."

And so we begin to see that these people, and all of us, have at one time or another been guilty of this very same thing. We begin to see that these people, and all of us, often fall into an academic understanding of the science. But we see that the deep innermost part of us is somehow or other in contest with it.

I think it is important that we realize that there are definite axioms of mind that are, in a sense, opposite to, or versus, or sometimes in contest with, the postulates of man. Think of that. The axioms of mind versus the postulates of man.

What is an axiom? An axiom, we know, with geometry,

and with our knowledge of mathematics, is a self-evident truth. An axiom is a truth which can be totally relied upon. An axiom is something that is not only a truth that can be relied upon, but its evidence is seen and it can be used. It is part of definite structure.

A postulate can sometimes be relied upon, but often it's simply a belief, an attitude, a thought structure that someone has when he is trying to oppose a truth or find out about a truth. And so man—you and I—is filled with the postulates, with the concepts and the thoughts, the possibilities that may be. We seem to be filled with maybe's. "Maybe it's true that there is a God. Maybe it's true that there is a law of mind. Maybe it's true that I can do something with myself. Maybe. But I'm really not so sure."

The axioms of mind are really the statements of the primal cause of God, of the Truth. The axioms of mind are that there is one Mind, one Power, one Presence, one Cause of all that is, one Source of being, one underlying indwelling Creative Action. This we know as an absolute truth. The opinions are something else.

William James, in a book called "Is Life Worthwhile?" says that there's risk behind everything. And then he says this: "Everything is predicated on maybe's, but faith often is the only thing that makes the result come true." Risk is in life. Everything is predicated on maybe's, but faith often is the only thing that makes the result come true. Now, where is faith? And what is that quality of faith that makes things come true? It must be knowledge, faith that is knowlege, that is a sure, clear, understanding of the axioms of mind, and not a person's consciousness confused by the postulates of mankind.

And so we begin to see that there is a three-stage action in life; three degrees, if you want to call it that. They are opinion, belief, and knowledge. Opinion is just the postulates of man; and it is an attitude, a thought, an experience, your point of view. A belief may be an axiom of mind or one of the postulates of man; it may be a combination of both. A belief is really what you are accepting as Truth in your life, or as a Truth for you. But knowledge—knowledge comes out of the heart and soul of the universe. In you and in me, knowledge is that understanding of the power and the presence of the good that is greater than we are that indwells us, that has brought us about, and which gives us energy and capability; it gives us the impulse, it even gives us the instinctual urge to achieve and to grow and to have that feeling of: "Yes! I can do this that the world says I probably cannot achieve."

Emerson, in his essay on worship, says, "We are born believing a man bears beliefs as a tree bears apples." Isn't that interesting? "We are born believing a man bears beliefs as a tree bears apples." So we are right back again to the very beginning of our lesson this morning.

What are we foreordained to? Are we foreordained to the old concepts or to that evolving, ongoing good that exists in the universe? And then, how is this good expressed? Through law. But what is the law? We said it was the law of belief. So we all come into this life with certain beliefs. And beliefs are implanted in us. And beliefs are sold to us. And we are educated into beliefs. And we bear these beliefs, as Emerson so beautifully said, "just as a tree bears apples." We are walking, talking, acting, functioning, belief-bearing beings.

What are you believing in? Where is your belief? There is a law of belief, and that is one of the primal statements in the Science of Mind. But you have to understand that the law of belief is really working all the time but can work as a law of knowledge if you begin to study and to understand yourself as an act of God. Then the laws of God, the axioms of mind for God, is Mind. The axioms of Infinite Consciousness are there ready to work in your life and in your experience.

Another quote, very interesting and directly related to this whole subject, is from Thoreau's Journal. He says, "We check and repress the divinity that stirs within us to fall down and worship the divinity that is dead without us." What is the divinity that is dead without us? The postulates of men; the belief structures of the human opinion; everything that says you are less than the child of God, less than the offspring of the Infinite Power and Presence, less than the capability to change and to grow and to become new, fresh, alive and forward-moving. That is the divinity that most people bow down to and worship: the lie about life.

So when we see that, what matters most is the way we think about life and the way we think about ourselves. And when I talk about God I'm really talking about an Infinite Intelligence, I'm talking about the spirit of life around us, and I'm talking about the spirit of life that is also within each one of us—ready, willing, very able, to work through us and to bring about the great good new thing. That is the evolutionary force, that to which we are foreordained, moving forward, progressing, and bringing about a new life, a new way of understanding.

And so it is not where we start that really matters so much, but it's what we do along the way. It's not your age. It's not the amount of study you have had. It is not the condition that you find yourself in. It's not anything in the realm of the postulates of men. It's your own consciousness; it's what you do with yourself; it's beginning to grasp the axioms of Mind.

Remember, the axioms of Mind are the Truths of being— that there is one life, that it is absolute power, that it is all good and beneficent, that it is infinite love forever giving that which it is, an evolving principle or law of good ever-unfolding, that it is your heritage, and if you choose to have knowledge of it, it becomes your destiny. What a glorious life! What a marvelous possibility! To think that we don't have to settle for the lesser. This is the strategy for the new life: To begin to divorce yourself from your old belief structures.

One of the questions that people often ask me is, "What are the pitfalls that a student of the Science of Mind could fall into?"

I always respond by saying, "Lack of awareness." By that answer I mean that they really are almost totally unaware of themselves as human beings. They are driven by forces within themselves. They drift. They are in a state of confusion. Everyone wants to be better and happier or more fulfilled. Unless you have a certain awareness of the physical condition, you cannot work with your mind to get a deeper awareness of that primal cause, that absolute good that is around and within you that can work through you, through awareness to change that physical world condition experience.

So lack of awareness is the pitfall—lack of awareness of what you are as a human being, of your problem, of your condition and lack of awareness of the axioms of Mind, of what your source is, of what primal cause is, of what God the good is.

I know a gentleman who was a total drifter. He was in a state of utter and complete confusion when I first saw him. He came into my office and said, "I haven't been working in a couple of years, I have odd jobs here or there, I don't know what to do, I'm just not sure about anything." And he happened to come into my office because someone had suggested that the Science of Mind might be helpful, that he should look into Religious Science. And so he came in really inquiring about Science of Mind, about what could happen to him. He was still very much in a state of confusion. After discussing with him the fact that he had to face up to the actuality of his being a drifter, of what that meant —not facing up to the challenges of his existence, not seeing and getting a sense of what he really liked, what he really desired, what his goals might be—as I moved his thinking from that awareness to an awareness of just a few of the axioms of Mind—that there is a power and a presence for good, it is in the universe and within him and that he could use it—as I moved him toward that, his eyes began to change. When he first came in, the confusion was so great that there was a glaze over his eyes and when I looked at him I really couldn't see him. But all of a sudden—you know how it is when you look at someone and sometimes you just get that real eye contact and it's a sort of a soul-to-soul, center-to-center, relationship—it happened right in my office. I saw him for the first time in that moment as the confusion began to dissolve.

I said, "You need a strategy for a new life, and it's right here if you choose to work with it and to use it." And he began a consistent study. He started our classwork, he came to whatever meetings he could during the week, he got guidance every once in a while from the teacher, and he began to apply the axioms of Mind into his life to get rid of many of the belief structures that were holding him back, that were bringing him confusion. These were the postulates of men. This was his parental upbringing, the condition of the environment in which he lived which was dreadful when I first met him. Within one year this man had a complete change. He had moved into the first real career job that he had ever had. And he began to develop it. This was a few years ago. And that man today has since moved into three different positions by choice, moving upward in his ongoing, forward-moving action in life.

We know that there is the possibility for change because that is what life is doing all the time. We are a voyage, not a harbor. We are in movement, we're not simply a condition. We have the possibility for growth and change if we accept the knowledge of the Truth. That liberates us.

Certainly "You shall know the truth and the truth shall make you free," because that freedom is freedom from the postulates of men, the beliefs and the opinions and the acceptances of men, and freedom for the knowingness of the knowledge of Truth that there is a power and a presence of good behind and within you, and that it can make for you a great and wonderful good life.

And so ends our lesson.

Dr. Stuart Grayson has been associated with the First Church of Religious Science in New York City for 14 years and is now the pastor of that church.

He pursued his ministerial studies under the direction of Dr. Raymond Charles Barker, who announced his plan to retire as minister of the New York Church in 1979.

Dr. Grayson has also studied privately with D. T. Suzuki, Alan Watts, and Swami Bodhananda. He has a great interest in Eastern and Western mysticism, both of which he has studied extensively.

In addition to his ministry, Dr. Grayson is a member of the Board of Directors of the International New Thought Alliance.

The talk, "Strategy for a New Life," was delivered by Dr. Grayson on February 25, 1979.

CHAPTER NINE

Thought is the seed of action; but action is as much its second form as thought is its first. It rises in thought, to the end that it may be uttered and acted. Always in proportion to the depth of its sense does it knock, importunately at the gates of the soul, to be spoken, to be done.

—Emerson

Self Resurrection

Reverend Richard J. Green

Here it is, Easter Sunday, and those of you who attend church regularly might be saying, "It's Easter Sunday. Here I am again. What's this guy going to talk about? What more can a minister say about Easter? It's all been said. We've heard it all. There's nothing new."

Well, there *is* something new. I have something very *new* to say about Easter.

My basic theme may be sort of a shocker to you, because it isn't necessarily what you are anticipating. Nonetheless, I have a fabulous Easter message today, and you will never guess what it's about.

It's about fat. F.A.T.

I want to be sure you hear the message from beginning to end, because if you don't hear the entire message, you may go home and tell your friends, "Well, he talked about cooking oil, or grease, or tummy bulges." But it isn't about

95

those things. It's about fat. There's a very important Easter message in F.A.T.

The parable of the prodigal son is an account of a young man who resurrected himself. He resurrected himself from a pigsty—by resurrecting his fat. F.A.T.

Now before I get into fat, I must define the word "resurrection." It means "to make alive again, or to bring back into view." The prodigal son *resurrected* himself from the pigsty. Returning home, his father met him half-way and said, "This is my beloved son, my son who was *dead* and is now alive."

We mustn't interpret the word "dead" to mean "void of the life in the physical body." We must interpret it as "one who is spiritually or mentally or emotionally dead."

Presently, none of us are physically dead, but there are times when we are emotionally or spiritually or mentally dead. But that's okay, because we can come alive again. Resurrection is "to bring to life again that which was dead;" and the process for Self resurrection is found in the word "fat."

Actually, what we are going to resurrect is found in the acronym "fat;" "F" meaning "feeling," "A" meaning "action," and "T" meaning "thought." If any or all are dead, we must resurrect them. When we resurrect Feeling, Action, and Thought, *we* come alive again.

Each of us is capable of Self resurrection. Say to yourself, "This is my 'Feeling, or Action, or Thought' which was dead and is now alive." Bringing back into life those three expressions becomes the Self resurrection.

Jesus stated that God is not a God of the dead but of the living. God is love, and those who are alive are loving what God is. Those who are dead are loving that which is the absence of God; those who are alive are loving absolute intelligence, unconditioned love, eternal life, perfect peace, unopposed power, undefiled beauty, profound joy.

Those who are dead love such things as lack, limitation, griping, pain, disease, helplessness, hopelessness, agonizing loneliness, bad news. They are subconsciously loving those particular circumstances, and what they love, they will experience!

To the degree that any man loves those qualities, they become his god—lack, limitation, and so on—whereas the God to those who are alive is Eternal Life and Unconditioned Love.

If we are spiritually, mentally, or emotionally dead, we must resurrect within ourselves the expression of Feeling, Action, and Thought.

We often feel, but we don't take action. Valentine's Day, perhaps, is designed for those who don't take action to express the words, "I love you," the other 364 days of the year. Maybe they think the words, maybe they feel them, but they don't normally take the action to express them; so Valentine's Day becomes an opportunity for expressing an action which is not often expressed.

We can feel and yet not express the action of our feelings. We often speak, without feeling. We often act, without thinking. Sometimes we think, without acting. There are many combinations that feelings, thoughts, and actions can fall into.

Since feelings, actions, and thoughts are a threesome, let's picture them as a triangle. If you remember your sophomore geometry, the three kinds of triangles are—the scalene, the isosceles, and the equilateral. The scalene triangle is the one in which all three angles are different from each other. Then, there's the isosceles triangle, and that one has two equal angles. The third kind is the equilateral triangle, and in that triangle, all angles are equal.

Recently I got out my little computer and did some figuring. I found something very interesting. On a scalene triangle, which would represent a triangle in which angles and sides are totally out of balance, no symmetry, there are about 300 angle combinations.

With the isosceles triangle, the one with two equal angles, there are about 100 combinations.

Then I questioned: How many angle combinations are there with an equilateral triangle? Here's what's exciting! The answer is *one*. One combination! We use the word "one" all the time: oneness, we are one-with. When we express oneness, that is a balanced expression, wherein we give equal expression to our thoughts, to our feelings, and to our actions. When feeling and action and thought are in balance in our expression, we are in balance.

Sometimes we tend to be lopsided. Perhaps we think, "I must become more intellectual," and then we subdue or inhibit feelings. We have been taught to believe that "as a man I must not express my feeling" because we remember our dad saying, "Little boys don't cry—be a man." As we inhibit our feelings, actions, or thoughts, we begin to become lopsided. We become like isosceles and scalene triangles. Our job right now is to resurrect all three expressions so that we will become totally balanced, totally symmetrical —equilateral.

How important is it to be symmetrical? We can find the answer in a parable by Jesus. Jesus told of a man who owned a vineyard and had two sons. The man said to the first son, "Will you go into the vineyard and help with the harvest?" And the son said, "No, I will not." But later he repented and went in. Then the man asked the second son, and the second son said, "Yes, I will." But he didn't.

Jesus then asked the people, "Which one of these sons did the will of the father?" The priests who considered themselves all-wise, said, "We know, we know! The one who went into the vineyard, he's the one who did the will of the father." And Jesus turned to them and said, "I say unto you, the publicans and the harlots will find the kingdom before you.''

That was quite a putdown, wasn't it? The answer, of course, is that *neither* of the sons expressed the will of the father. The will of the father is simply this: THE KINGDOM OF HEAVEN IS HARMONY, AND THERE'S NO WAY THAT ANYONE WHO IS IN OPPOSITION TO ONE'S SELF CAN ENTER THE KINGDOM OF HEAVEN. The point to be made is this: to think one way and to express its opposite is Self opposition. Anyone filled with opposition can't enter into harmony.

Therefore, when you're feeling but not speaking, when you're acting but not thinking, you're in opposition with yourself. And that opposition will keep you out of the kingdom of heaven. It is only when we express in the equilateral sense—Feeling, Action, and Thought, all in balance, all harmonious—that we will enter into the kingdom of heaven. Who then does the will of the father? The individual who thinks and feels and acts in perfect harmony with himself. There are many times, however, when we don't do it.

Here is an example of a person whose fear colored his thinking and impeded his action. A man leaving Canada entered the freeway in the State of Washington, going the wrong direction. For 25 miles he raced down the freeway dodging the oncoming cars. The highway patrol was called out. Officers in helicopters using loudspeakers shouted down to the man. All of the other drivers on the road were dodging this man; everyone assumed that there was a lunatic in that car. Finally, the driver was pulled over. He was approached with great caution because the officers suspected that inside that car was a very sick man. Then this nice guy jumped out of the car and said, "Boy, am I ever glad to get out of that mess! It was terrible. It scared me half to death." The troopers said, "You're sane, you sound like a rational man." The man said, "Yeah, I'm okay." They asked him, "Why did you drive for 25 miles on the wrong side of the freeway? Didn't you think of turning off?" He answered, "You bet I thought about turning off! I thought about it constantly, but every time I came to one of those exits, there was a sign that said STOP, GO BACK, ONE WAY, DO NOT ENTER."

That funny but true story depicts a man who distorted his ability to think and impeded his ability to act. At that particular time, his feelings, his actions, and his thinking were not balanced. He wasn't equilateral.

Do you recall I mentioned recently a story about a woman on a boat, in New York City, who fell overboard and the other passengers simply stood there watching? How many times do we read today of individuals being in accidents or great peril and other people just watching? Many people today tend to impede their ability to take action. They think. They feel. But are they taking any action? The events in our life and of society often impede our ability to take action. But to the degree that we don't take action, to the degree that we don't think, to the degree that we don't feel, we remain unbalanced and are never going to enter the kingdom of heaven.

We could ask, "Who had done the will of the Father?" (Remember, the will of the Father is simply: that we inherit the kingdom). The answer is: those who think and feel and act in a congruent sense, in which their ability to feel, think, and act tends to be equal. Those who feel and act and think in unbalanced proportions cannot enter that kingdom and in no way execute the will of the Father.

If we picture an equilateral triangle, we know that regardless of how large it is, every equilateral triangle that is smaller will fit into it easily. Picture an equilateral triangle of one size and then a smaller one fitting in, and another and another and another; as they get smaller in size yet greater in number, they all fit perfectly. That's how we enter the kingdom of heaven. The kingdom of heaven is an infinitely large equilateral triangle.

Put your equilateral triangle inside the Infinite one. That's what it means to be congruent with God. But if we are an isosceles triangle or a scalene triangle, we cannot fit. Not because there's some grumpy old man with a beard in a nightgown with a big book recording "sins" and not because a voice says, "You aren't worthy; you can't enter this place." It is because Principle mandates, "You do not fit." What's the old cliche? "You can't put a square peg in a round hole." Well, an isosceles triangle won't fit into an equilateral triangle. It doesn't matter how "good" it is or how "bad" it is. It just won't fit. That's a Principle. And that's what we need to understand about the kingdom of heaven.

I feel for those who go to church just because it's Easter Sunday and think, "Aha. God is watching, and I'm going to get a brownie point. Because I'm in church on Easter Sunday, I'm going to fit into the kingdom of heaven." I'd like to see them try. No one is going to fit into the kingdom until they are an equilateral triangle, until their thoughts and their feelings and their actions become congruent with God. What *we* must do is resurrect our ability to think and to feel and to act.

Can you think of yourself as being prosperous? Yes! Why there's really nothing that should keep us from thinking that. Or is there? You have to answer that question yourself. Can you *feel* and *think of* yourself as being a prosperous person? Can you *act* as though you are a prosperous person?

We all have read those neat prosperity books that we have back on the book table. We buy prosperity books and get so excited. But often what we construct from such books is a scalene triangle, in which we think and think and think about prosperity, but we don't feel prosperous, and in no way do we act the least bit prosperous. Only when we *think* and *feel* and *act* prosperous will we truly be prosperous.

How about loving? Can you think of yourself as a loving person? *Do* you think of yourself as a loving person? Are you thought of by others as a loving person? Do you feel yourself filled with love this moment? If so, what are you doing with it? We need to take action. The action is vital.

How about alive? We think of ourselves as being alive as contrasted with the so-called living death. But how much aliveness is in you? How much life is there? How spirited are you? Are we zombies? Or are we truly alive? Can you think of yourself as really being alive? Do you think other people are thinking (of you), "What an alive person! What a dynamic individual! What an energetic being!"? Do you think of yourself that way? Can you feel yourself being that way? Try it now. Try right now to feel within yourself the feeling of being alive. We feel life. Let's be more enthusiastic about life. And what action can we take? The action that we can take is to stand up a little straighter. Smile more broadly. We can radiate totally. We *can* take action.

Isosceles triangles are formed by a person who is not taking action. That tiny acute angle at the top is the result of no action. Or perhaps, no feeling. An acute angle isn't cute!

How about joyful? Have you thought of yourself as a joyful person? Can you feel yourself being a joyful person? Ask yourself: "Am I a joyful person? Am I filled with joy?"

There's a neat term that I like to use: Filled full. We often say, "Well, I'm fulfilled. Yes, I went to the lecture and it fulfilled my needs." That's what we say when we want to be polite. But when we are filled full, we really have something. I don't want to be fulfilled, because to be fulfilled isn't enough. The word sounds as though you have a lot, but some "fulfilled people" are empty. Let's be filled full, filled full with joy, happiness, and love! Can you think of yourself that way? Can you feel yourself that way? And can you take the action to be that way? Resurrect the F.A.T.

How many times, when we were in school, did we have an opportunity to stand on a stage in front of people? We were given the chance to go up to the stage and read the speech or the poem or whatever, but we couldn't do it. We couldn't take the action. "Not me. They won't get me up there. I'll never do that sort of thing." This is the inability to take action, and it's the product of self opposition.

Keep in mind how we use the word "poise." In my opinion, it is one of the greatest words in our language. It means "to in no way be opposed to yourself." Isn't that a fabulous way to be? Who is your own worst enemy? Usually it's yourself; but when you're poised, you're in no way in opposition to yourself. Think of yourself as a poised person. Feel yourself as a poised person. And then act as a poised person.

Emerson wrote, "If you don't have a virtue, assume it and you will have it." We often think, "I'll sit here and wait, and as soon as I feel poised or I sense something, I'll do it." Then we wait. Well, "He who hesitates is lost" or "He who hesitates is last." Let's take the action, assume the virtue.

How about one with God? Can you think of yourself as one with God? Perhaps we think everyone else is one with God. Some people may say, "Well, Jesus was one with God." Others, you know, can be one with God too. Can you be? "No, not me," you say? Why not? You *are* one with God. Think of yourself as being one with God. God is life, and there's life in you. The life that you feel *is* God. Really think it. Truly feel it. Sincerely act it. And then, should there be difficulties, or when there are challenges in your life, turn to that center and feel that ONENESS with God, and anticipate the kingdom of harmony.

There is one more thing that needs to be said about Self Resurrection. Tension is the result of unexpressed feeling.

When we have feelings and we don't express them, tension is produced. Have you ever been at work and the boss says, "Come on, work harder, you're falling behind"? Do you feel that tension growing and growing and growing, and your jaw getting tighter and tighter and tighter? When you go to lunch, do you say through clenched teeth, "I'll have soup because I can't open my jaw!"? And when you go home and your sweetie says, "Hi, honey, did you have a nice day?" do you answer, through clenched teeth, "Yes, I had a wonderful day." We hold our feelings in because we don't know the proper way to release them, but this inhibition causes a totally *new* problem. We have a lot of good feelings. We need to release the good feelings too. We have, however, the habit of inhibiting. We inhibit all feelings, good and bad. There are times when we need to inhibit the bad feelings. But why inhibit the good feelings? To inhibit feelings is to cause tension.

Stress usually is the result of our inability to take the action prompted by our feelings. We don't act, we can't act. We need to take action. Perhaps we need to make a phone call. Perhaps we need to do some kind of physical activity, but we don't do it. Remember, the stress in your life is, for the most part, from the lack of action—the inability to respond to your feelings.

Look at yourself now, and if you find that tension is one of the major challenges in your life, perhaps you're not expressing your feelings. If stress is in your life, perhaps you are not expressing the actions that you would like to express.

If vacillation is one of the major conflicts in your life, start thinking for yourself, because vacillation is the result of not thinking.

Don't be a non-thinker. Don't be a non-feeler. Don't be a non-actor. Think and feel and act.

This Easter message calls for resurrecting of your Feeling, Action, and Thought. And you can do it, starting right now. They need to be resurrected. If you will resurrect F.A.T., then you understand perfectly the Scripture, in which, when the prodigal son returned home, the father said, "Look, for this is my son who was *dead* and is *alive* again. He was lost and is found." And they began to be merry.

When you resurrect your Feelings and your Actions and your Thoughts, *you* will be that which is alive again, that which was lost and is found. And *you* will find that you and your whole universe will begin to be merry. Do this and you will have the merriest Easter that you've ever experienced.

Reverend Richard J. Green has been a minister for 4 years, during which time he has been the minister of the Los Gatos, California Church of Religious Science.

Prior to his ministerial training, which was completed under the direction of the late Dr. Chet Castellaw, he taught in public schools and community colleges for more than 20 years.

Reverend Green is a regular contributor to Creative Thought Magazine. In addition, he has authored 3 works: "Meditation, the Highway to Happiness," "Dissolving Depression and Finding Peace," and "A Nest of Pleasant Thoughts."

The talk, "Self Resurrection," was given by Reverend Green at the Los Gatos church on April 15, 1979.

CHAPTER TEN

Life is discovering what we like, learning more about life and finding a way to share it with other people.
We start by finding out where we are in mind, what we believe about ourselves and the dimensions and priorities of our lives.
We then set out to make the changes we want. It's a sort of Truth in Labeling Law.

—Harrold

Being Positively Selfish

Reverend Leslie Scott Harrold

Being positively selfish is: "Being," just being right here and right now, in the here and now; "Positive" means running your own life in the direction of life in a positive, forward, moving way, from the here and now moving forward; "Selfish" means really involved with one's self, but not from an egotistical selfish standpoint. You see, the selfish person in our old definition of it means "one who gets." The selfish person that I'm talking about is "one who gives." That's the difference. Positive selfishness is a characteristic of a self-oriented person who knows that life is a process of unfolding itself. Life is a process of discovering what it is that you like to do, discovering all about that and sharing that with other people. That is being positively selfish.

I have evolved some techniques I want to share with you that have to do with the personal evolution of one's self and how to go about this process of discovering what it is you like and then developing that, and then sharing it with other people.

I'll take a step back here and make a quick review, because it lays down a foundation for what I want to talk about. The thing that we're doing is a process of self-discovery. If you're here, that means you're committed to self-discovery, the self-development. That is the foundation, that's the base upon which we all gather together here. Having committed ourselves to learn something about ourselves and self-developing, we recognize that we do move from where we are to where we want to be. I refer to that as "Here we are in game plan 1." And that game plan has a certain dimensional definition to it. It's constituted of friends, of spouses, children, relatives, jobs, hobbies, fulfillments, escapes, material things; and that game plan we came from, you see, is constituted of that dimension. These outer dimensions of game plan 1 that we're living or moving from are based upon beliefs that we hold, because everything we experience in life is a reflection of a state of belief that we have in mind. So now we come along and we tell our own mind that we're going to leave this game plan because we want self-development. We want to have more of life, to enjoy more of life, to be more prosperous, healthy, happy, loving, and all that; and we're going to move from this game plan to a new one. But the point I make—this is a very valid point—is that instead of just simply redefining the new game plan in the same type of terms as the game plan we just left, let's do it a different way. Let's define the dimensions of the new game plan in terms of the qualities of God: love, fulfillment, perfect self-expression, personal physical well-being, personal material well-being, happiness, joy, self-expression. All of the qualities that you feel to be the qualities of God are then the parameters of the new game plan, not the specific things but the parameters in terms of the qualities of God, making these qualities not standards you have to live up to but rather qualities to live from. Then, every day, say, "All right, the qualities of my life are the God qualities, they are my qualities now. They constitute love, happiness, joy, fulfillment, self-expression, perfect health, prosperity." Whatever you say it is. Say, "All right, now, Mind, or God, let me experience *that,* today, this day. Let me move from that. Not something I have to live up to."

You know, we put these standards upon ourselves. Let us put no standard upon ourselves, make no definition of how that's going to come about, but rather just stand right in the middle of it and say, "Okay, fine, show me what that's like today. Let me experience those God qualities that are my qualities now. Let me experience that today, through me, as me." Then just go right ahead and do it. That's the foundation.

In my own continuing self-exploration and self-confrontation, I took this a step further, an interesting step. I said— as I left this game plan here, game plan 1—that I could perceive that this game plan had a certain dimension to it while I'm saying that the new game plan has a different kind of a definition, the God-qualities definition. That's not going to stop me from just operating right now. But, realistically, looking at it just very practically and without any self-delusion about it, I said, "Okay, now, here's what I think that I came from. Now, Mind, tell me what I really believe the dimensions of my life to be right now. What are the dimensions of my life?" The very first word that came out—and the way I work is with a piece of paper and a pencil so when I ask my mind a question like that I am prepared to write down the answers as they come out—the first thing that came out was something quite surprising to me. I honestly don't want to share what it was with you, but it was a surprise, something I absolutely did not expect to be the first word.

But my mind then came up with a definition of what I believe the dimensions of my life to be right now. If I am truly going to move from here to this new game plan that is defined in the terms of the God qualities, I want to know where I'm starting from, and I want to accept that just the way it is. I cannot make this step if I do not accept where I am. You can say, "I should be there." Well, if you really and truly should be there, you'd be there. But I needed a definition of where I am, so I just simply asked my mind, "Okay, mind, what is the dimension of my life right now?" That's the first meditative approach that I want to share with you. Then I got that down. That got to be twenty single words that constituted the outline, or dimension, of my life. I got that down. I got it on paper anyway. It may scare me to do anything about it but at least I got the thing pinned down, and I can do something about it when I want to.

The second thing I did, I asked my mind—"Okay, that's fine, now let's go at it a different way. Give me the priorities that I now have in my life. What are my priorities?" That was surprising too, because the priorities that I have inside of my own belief structure were different from what I thought they were. I used a piece of paper. You don't have to use a piece of paper. The important thing is that you move from your subconscious mind to your conscious awareness, the dimension of the priorities of your life. What does your life consist of? What is it? What's its diameter? What's its circumference? What's its center point? And, the priorities you have determine how you're going to act. Regardless of how you think you're going to act, you're going to act in accordance with your dominant priorities. If you find yourself going a certain way and you're telling yourself you want to go another way, you set up an automatic stress-producing situation within your own self. So find out the dimension of your life and find out the priorities.

The next step was to recognize that many times most of us are constantly operating by a system of choices between things. We say we should be a certain way—and that's based on our history, our past, our upbringing, our society, our culture, and the race history, and all of that. Rarely, except for people like you and me who are in Religious Science, do people confront their own selves with their own intelligence, submitting the experiences of their lives to their own intelligence. Instead, people set up a system of "should" and "have to" and then try to live life. We're constantly setting up these things where we go this way for a little while and say something like, "I should be doing this, I'll quit smoking." And pretty soon you're back smoking again, and then you say, "Oh, I shouldn't do that." This is called the horns of the dilemma. We are always between the horns of the dilemma, making choices between two things. I'm saying, with this process of finding out the dimensions of life and what priorities you have, you get in total agreement with yourself; good, bad, or indifferent.

Agree on where you are, not making any judgment on where you are, just being in total agreement with yourself. Now, here's an interesting way to do that. Have the courage to make another list. Ask yourself, "What do I consider to be my negative qualities? What is it that I do not like about me?" You know, that's surprising. Do you want to do something interesting? Make a list of what you think to be your negative qualities and make a list of what you think to be your positive qualities, and guess which list will be longer. The negative ones, sure. We're set up to self-flagellate. That means to beat ourselves. I've studied enough history to know that the history of religion, the history of theology, will show you why we are set up to self-flagellate. Who cares? Who cares how it came about? What difference does it make? The point is we're here and we're now. Make a list of your negative qualities. Then comes the fun part. Convert every negative quality to a new label, a new positive label. You see, what we do in life is walk around with our little pocketful of labels, we observe something we're doing, we take a label out of our pocket, write a negative statement on it, stick it on the event, and then we try to deal with the label. That's insane; we created it in the first place. So make a list of all the negative qualities that you can think of about yourself. And that's easy to do. I'll guarantee you that that's easy.

Once you've got the negative qualities pinned down, then you just re-label them, that's all. The negative label is an opinion anyway, just an opinion. So you just erase that opinion and put in a new opinion, put on a positive label. Call it your "Truth in Labeling Law."

All right, let's take some examples. You say, "Well, I'm uptight." Convert that to "I'm concerned." That feels better. "I'm stubborn. No, I'm not. I'm determined." "I'm emotionally unstable. No. I'm sensitive." You know, it doesn't make any difference to mind. Mind will respond to what you say it is. So why not convert every negative about yourself? Just put a new label on it and act from the new label; deal with yourself from the new label. What's wrong with that? That's pretty neat. That's the most valuable thing you'll hear today. The one thing Religious Science persons do is learn how to work with time. A lot of people say, "I waste a lot of time." How would you convert that negative? That could be "I'm thoughtful." You see, once you get a positive list instead of a negative list going, mind, that is, the creative aspect of our being, must respond in experience based upon that new labeling system. It's got to.

That is the nature of the creative process. God endowed us with a creative process and that's how it works. The creative process works by bringing into our experience what we give ourselves to work with. That's really a very freeing concept because that puts us firmly in charge of our own experience, and that's what we want.

So I guess in summary here, what I am saying is that, yes, we all want to grow. We do. There is a divine urge within us that just simply is operating at all times. We do want to grow. Life does get better. Life is getting better. We do want to move from game plan 1 to game plans 2 and 3, and infinitely. We want to continue the process of self-development because we have come to an understanding in our approach to Truth that life is a process of exploring ourselves, finding out about ourselves, and sharing that with the world, with other people. So we do want to grow. We know that as we grow we have more and more of ourselves to give. And as we give we make room for the receiving also. We let life experience us, and we experience life. We give and we receive, because that's the way life is. And to do so, we deal here in this particular church with some very practical means.

Define the dimension of your life as you see it now, as it is now in your belief structure, by asking your own mind what you really believe to be the dimensions of your life. Ask yourself what your priorities in life are. Then ask yourself to give yourself a list of the negative qualities, and convert that negative list into a list of positive qualities. You might do that first, because what I'm getting to is that once you have the definition of the dimension of your life and have your own list of priorities, the question becomes what to do about it.

The simplest answer on what to do about it once you've got all your negatives converted, once you have the definition of where you are, and once you have a knowledge about where the priorities in your life are, I truly believe that the easiest thing to do is this: Just get up every morning—or don't get up, whatever—take some period of time, and it doesn't have to be very long, and tell yourself that the qualities of God are love, health, personal well-being, personal physical feeling good, prosperity, personal material well-being, happiness, joy, fulfillment, perfect self-expression, wholeness, the balanced wholeness in life, and say to yourself, "That's it." And that's a statement of Truth. Your mind can't argue with that, because that is a statement of truth. Can your mind say, "Oh, yeah?" No, because your mind has to know that that statement of the qualities of God is a statement of truth. Your mind can't argue with that. Just say, "Okay. This is it. Show me today. Now." And then just let the day progress through you, through the expression of those qualities of God.

If everybody did that, we would live in a world so beautiful and happy and prosperous. There would be no war, no poverty. It would be tranquil, yet active. It would be very beautiful. We would all see each other in the light of the God qualities. We would share with one another. We would be able to receive from other persons. We would know that they were giving out of the qualities of God. We would just be able to open up and receive abundant good in our lives and give it. We would eliminate pollution, we'd work on that right away, that would be simple. We would eliminate dependence on any other person in our relationships or in the national or worldwide picture. We would eliminate fear. We would eliminate illness, because there'd be nothing to get sick about. We would eliminate poverty and move forward into a world of such beauty. We have it within us right here and now, today, to do that.

So let's be very positively selfish and get on with it. And so it is.

Reverend Leslie Scott Harrold gave his talk, "Being Positively Selfish," on February 25, 1979 at the Church of Religious Science, San Clemente, California. He has been pastor of that church since 1973, the year in which he began his ministry. His 4 years of preparatory study were taken at the Church of Religious Science, Monterey, California with Dr. Oscar Pitcock.

Reverend Harrold's business background is extensive, encompassing 25 years in industry. In those years, he held managerial or supervisorial positions in personnel management, industrial relations, marketing, purchasing and public relations. Six of his technical articles have been published in personnel management journals. Teaching is also a part of Reverend Harrold's background. He has held a California Teaching Credential, Secondary Level, endorsed for Psychology; and he wrote all of the training material for the "Psychology of Every Day Living" course which he taught.

In addition to being the pastor of the San Clemente Church, Reverend Harrold is the Regional Director of RSI for the Southern California Region and a member of the Executive Committee for RSI youth programs. He has instructed all of the 4 years of accredited classes plus developing and presenting some 25 special classes and seminars in Science of Mind.

CHAPTER ELEVEN

*Act well at the moment, and you have performed
a good action for all eternity.*

—Lavater

Do You Act or React?

Dr. Mildred C. Hinckley

Do you act or do you merely react?

This is a very important area of personal analysis. If you merely react, you are constantly at the mercy of people and situations. If you are one who acts, you are free to establish your own mental atmosphere and activity.

I've often touched on this idea of acting or reacting, but it is of such importance in our lives—to our happiness and success—that I believe it is worth thinking about together once in a while. It is interesting to me that whenever I speak on this subject, or refer to it, I receive much comment from you on the lesson; and you seem to remember it longer than other talks. Maybe two years from now somebody will come to me and say, "Do you act or react?" And that makes me very happy.

I doubt if any of us realizes how much of the time we are merely reacting to the flow of life and to the conditions in the world of form and to the mental atmosphere around us. That is not the path of individual expression or creativity; you were not created to be merely a sounding-board. You were created to be a precious, highly individual, indispensable expression of God in your world and affairs—a creator. You were created to sing your own song in harmony and unison with the song celestial, the harmony of the spheres; and when you are doing that, you will be adding your note to the symphony of life, you will be in harmony, and you will be happy and productive.

When people are busy expressing God in themselves, when they are singing their own song, they have neither time nor inclination to react to less than the wholeness and beauty and goodness of God. When each one is busy singing his own song, he will discover he is in harmony and in unison with the symphony of life.

A symphony is made up of the contributing parts of each instrument. They blend, they work together, but each makes its own distinct, valuable contribution. The winds don't say, "We are the most important." The strings don't say, "No, we are the most important." The percussions don't boom back, "You are wrong. Where would you be without us?" Each plays its own important part, sometimes in solo, sometimes in unison, interacting harmoniously with each other.

I am convinced that most of the woes of the world would be eliminated if the principle involved here could be activated, if every person were trained to sing his own song and to realize the value and importance of his contribution to life. Instead, people so often just react to a good or bad situation in which they find themselves. They do not initiate action. Their reaction may be a loud outcry against the existing condition. They may suffer, criticize, blame, and even try to extricate themselves; however, all the time they are just reacting. They haven't done anything creative or personally significant. Their response is solely to the outside stimuli. It doesn't originate within themselves.

Do you act or merely react? Now, there is nothing wrong

with reacting if one does not lose his individual initiative and conscious choice. In fact, it is very important that we are capable of responding. Do we say, "But do I *choose* to react? Is this something to which I choose to respond?" Or do we say with Paul: "None of these things moves me. I do not choose to be moved by these things so I may finish my course with joy"? Those are the words of an initiator of action. Those are the words of one who acts. And he influences the events and the flow of life around him. If you remember, Paul was in deep trouble when he made his declaration. His very life was in the balance, and he knew it. The Jews were screaming for his blood. But he chose to remain unmoved.

When one stands in the midst of a negative or challenging situation and refuses to react to the appearance, one becomes a positive force for good, for harmony, for right action. The term "right action" is frequently used in Religious Science. To me, it is one of the most freeing acceptances of the divine idea that we can make. Humanly we do not always know the right course of action, the right or divine solution. But there is a *perfect mind within us* that does know the right answer to every problem, the answer that is right for all concerned. This takes my *human opinion* or anyone else's *limited ideas* entirely out of the situation.

Do you realize how free such an attitude can make you? You can be a deliberate and positive cause to your world. You would not need to spend your life reacting to everything around you—whether the thing is good, bad, or indifferent—and suffering or experiencing the mental and emotional and physical consequences of each action. You are the one who can decide *how* you respond to an experience.

We in Fillmore had a dramatic illustration of this in our own city when the devastating flood of last year left hundreds of our people homeless. Some of the victims were completely desolate. Others were not. The whole community rose up and there was an outpouring of caring and loving help such as I have never seen before in my experience—and I am glad to think about it again. Help and loving concern poured in from all over the country. One small example: Four of the members of our local Soroptomist Club lost practically everything. Several thousand dollars came immediately to them from other clubs in the organization across the nation. People opened up their homes. Others spent endless hours with shovels helping to clear away the mud. People from far beyond our community came to help with the mountainous job of clearing away the three to four feet of mud left by the flood.

But here's the crux of this illustration for us this morning. Every person involved had the privilege of choosing how he or she would react. One man who lost everything said to me, "This is the most wonderful experience of my life. I suddenly have a sense of values I have never had before. Material things do not matter, but the loving caring of people for people that is going on here does!" That man chose his response to a community and personal catastrophe, and for him it became a lifting, spiritual experience.

When you have learned to be the one who acts—I could say an actor, but I don't mean a performer—when you have learned to be the one who acts or initiates action, mental or physical, in your own mind and affairs, you can choose that to which you respond intelligently and deliberately; and it's wonderful. For instance, you choose to react to beauty and you begin to see beauty everywhere. There are people who go through life blind to the beauty that surrounds them. I know people who could drive from here to Ventura, a road that is absolutely bathed in beauty, and seldom get beyond the contemplation of "Aunt Minnie's latest operation," the terrible state of politics, the crisis that is brewing at the office; or they might go along and their eyes may pick out everything that is unsightly. All of this is reaction. But it is not trained, directed, purposeful reaction.

To the one who chooses what it is that he is going to react to, the world becomes a wonderful place. He cultivates the habit of seeing and responding to the beautiful and true, not to the ugly and negative. Both are there to see, but if he is a self-conscious chooser he chooses to see and respond to the good, because that is the pleasant and happy thing to do. That kind of responding pays the biggest dividends in personal satisfaction and fulfillment.

The same thing is true about our contact with other people. What do you choose to react to in them? If you are making a conscious choice you will in all probability respond to the best and not to the worst. If you are merely reacting you will respond to the *entire* personality of the individual; and this is a good way to lose friends and be influenced by people—because, how many people do you know who do not have something irritating or downright aggravating about them? You each have ten fingers. Count off on your fingers the people you know well who have no irritating faults. Go ahead and count them, I'll give you a minute. You may have one or two saints on your list but I doubt it; there aren't very many of those around right now.

When my husband and I were married, nobody cried at the wedding. They laughed. They didn't quite clap, but almost—because both of our families had given up hope that either of us would ever find anyone that would be willing to put up with us. But somehow it lasted. I think it's going to be a meaningful relationship. It's because we wanted it to be. I guess each of us was so grateful to find someone willing to put up with us that the good traits in the other were magnified. We each chose to hold reaction to the irritating qualities of the other to a minimum and to disregard them completely when we could. He is not time-conscious. So what? Maybe he's right and I'm the one with the irritating sense of time. You know, it's quite a thing when one of us is always fifteen minutes early and the other one is fifteen minutes late. That takes a little working on. We choose to react to, concentrate on, and enjoy the commendable qualities in each other. Each of us in this respect is an actor, not merely a reactor. I doubt if any marriage could be happy or perhaps even survive unless it is based on the determination of the partners to respond to the best in each other.

Do you read the letters to newspaper columnists asking for advice? It is something of an education. It is a revelation to read about the insignificant, and often asinine, complaints about their mates which are so annoying to some people that they are driven to the desperation of turning to a public counselor for advice. Another law is called into action here; it concerns a couple's focusing only on the things to which they are willing to give attention and responding only to the best in each other. It is the power of praise. It is sheer magic. What is praised unfolds and it flourishes. What is ignored, overlooked, or minimized, diminishes. If there be any virtue, if there be any praise, for heaven's sake talk about these things.

I knew a man who married a cynical, cold "old maid," an expression that was used years ago. He saw qualities in her that I'm sure she didn't see in herself. He told her how lovely she was—how beautiful, how warm, and how affectionate she was. Through his eyes of love she must have looked that way to him. He never stopped telling her these things, which were the truth about her real self. The truth about her real self was not the hard shell of false ideas she had drawn around herself and the face that she showed to the world. This man knew nothing about the Science of

Mind, but he was practicing the truth intuitively. It didn't happen overnight, but the day came when other eyes besides his saw his wife as beautiful, warm, affectionate, and loving. He had melted all the ice away, and there indeed was the girl that he had seen all the time.

While we're talking about people's reaction to people, let's talk about individuals. Individuals are people too. You know, it's very easy to talk in the "people-people" way, but it's a little bit more demanding to think about it in personal terms.

People are constantly reacting to themselves. They create a self-image that dominates and colors their thinking and emotions, and that image is thus the determining factor in their experience. Their self-image tells them they can or they can't do this or that. They seldom confront themselves with the challenge, "Am I acting or am I merely reacting? Am I reacting to a limiting thought pattern that I have convinced myself is me? Or am I choosing what I think about myself? Do I see myself as a strong, worthy child of God? Or do I settle for a self-image of weakness, inferiority, or frustration?"

Everyone should read "Psycho-Cybernetics" by Maltz at least one time. It will give you a much clearer picture of how you live with yourself as an actor or merely a reactor. How you react to yourself can make all the difference between being a happy, healthy, well-adjusted person or being half alive, missing the enjoyment of possibilities that are rightfully yours.

One of the most important facets of the subject this morning—one that much of our happiness, success, and certainly our peace of mind, depends on—is the way we react to situations. I touched on that a few minutes ago when I was talking about the flood. We all move from one situation or experience to another; good, fine, positive, constructive situations, or seemingly negative challenging experiences. We encounter interesting, happy events and those that can bring sorrow and pain. We are constantly moving into relationships with people and places and things, from the most casual to the most demanding. This is the way of life. These experiences and personal relationships are with other people who are very human—not many of them know yet that they are divine, and not too many of them act like they are. Often our experiences are with people who are under stress and who do and say things that they would not do under less trying conditions. Sometimes we are in situations where the motivation of other people involved is not good. But this is not the rule. Most people, no matter how "human" they may seem to be, have an inner decency about them that will respond when recognized. What I'm saying is: All of us live in a continuing chain of events, conditions, and situations; how we meet this flow of varying experience determines the quality of our lives.

Do we sing our own song? It may come as a surprise to anyone who has not thought it through that one does not have to react emotionally at all to a situation unless one chooses to react. If this were not so, all doctors and nurses would be totally devastated and there could not be a happy doctor or a happy nurse. The sights and sounds to which they are constantly exposed would devour them and they would die young untimely deaths. But this is not so. Most doctors and nurses I know are as happy and well-adjusted as people in other occupations and professions. Take morticians for example. They deal constantly with sorrow and death. Yet those I've known have been as happy and well-adjusted as most people. These people's professions necessitate that they do not respond to the emotional stresses to which they are constantly exposed. They are interested, compassionate, understanding, and dedicated. But they cannot react. They *must* not. Or they could not stay in these fields and maintain their own well-being. They learn to put what might be called a psychic shield around themselves— "circle of light" is the way I think about it. Paul called it the armor of light. They choose not to react. They cannot respond or they would cease to be effective. A grieving, weeping mortician would not be able to give the calm, pleasant assistance and service that people need at that time.

Ministers and practitioners also have to learn this very quickly or they do not stay long in their professions either. People go to a doctor for his good advice, and the strength and assurance of his very attitude can help them. A good doctor can heal a person by just walking into the room. A pleasant, helpful nurse is about the most comforting creature God ever made. A long-faced, concerned nurse can give a sick person or his family the willies.

That reminds me of a classic and what is now a most amusing story of such a nurse in our family history. It was not very funny when it was happening. Our boy, our only child, was born six weeks premature. The delivery went on into the night. As the hours crept by, my husband Lawrence was beside himself with anxiety—that was before he was a Religious Scientist. He was sitting alone in the waiting room chewing his fingernails as the hours dragged on towards one o'clock in the morning. Finally he heard footsteps echoing in the hall upstairs and then coming slowly down the stairs. The lights were low. There wasn't a sound except for those slowly approaching, slightly echoing footsteps. He jumped up and met the nurse as she reached the foot of the stairs. Her face was white and solemn, and in a hoarse whisper she said, "Mr. Hinckley, the doctor wishes to see you at the end of the hall upstairs." Lawrence took the stairs two at a time. When he reached the top, all was in darkness except for a weak little light at the end of the hall. He could see the doctor in his white uniform just standing there. At that moment, I was in grave danger of becoming a widow and a mother simultaneously. Lawrence bounded down the hall and the doctor looked at him with a big smile and said, "Mr. Hinckley, you are the father of a fine boy."

If the nurse had just smiled and said, "Mr. Hinckley, the doctor has some interesting news for you, he's waiting to see you upstairs," how different Lawrence would have felt. That nurse was really a nice girl; but she had a very pale complexion, she never smiled, and everything was very very serious. And she just about scared my husband out of his wits.

I would say that Lawrence reacted, wouldn't you?

Today I think it would be different. If it happened today at my age I think he would drop dead. The media would all be there and I would be famous, a Twentieth Century Sarah.

Well, if Lawrence had been a practicing Religious Scientist as he is today, I know it would have helped. He would have been sitting there endeavoring to quietly treat and realize that perfect right action was taking place, that God was the only activity and power, that only right and perfect and beautiful fulfillment was manifesting. He would have been in such a poised state of mind that he could not have been ready to jump at a negative conclusion, at a false impression as given by this solemn-faced nurse.

The next time you are in a demanding situation that seems to be negative, simply refuse to act or react. Just stand still and think, "God is right here in the midst of it. God is right here. God is all good. I refuse to respond to any appearance of the negative. I choose not to respond to this situation. I am the one who acts, who chooses what I think and what I feel." In this way, your mind will be clear and calm, and you will be ready to take whatever outer action is indicated. You will not be panicked. You will be the actor—the one who acts.

You will be singing your own song in harmony with the symphony of life.

Dr. Mildred C. Hinckley is presently the pastor of the Fillmore Church of Religious Science, Fillmore, California, which she established.

Previous to her association with the Fillmore church, Dr. Hinckley was active in founding the First Religious Science Church in Ventura, California. She served on the board and was active in teaching.

Her ministerial studies were taken with Dr. Robert H. Bitzer. She also studied with Dr. Dan Custer.

Dr. Hinckley's professional background and interests, in other than religious activities, include newspaper and promotional work. She was the manager of an art gallery at one time, and she is currently a member of Soroptomist International.

Twenty-three years ago Dr. Hinckley became active in Religious Science. However, she studied religious philosophy for many years prior to that time. In addition to her ministry of 15 years, she has served as a board member of RSI.

"Do You Act or React?" was presented by Dr. Hinckley at the Fillmore church on March 18, 1979.

CHAPTER TWELVE

This is the beginning.

— Johnson

The Letter of Truth

Dr. Tom Johnson

Basically, when we talk about the "letter" we mean consciously, deliberately, knowing the truth, consciously using the Science of Mind to demonstrate whatever it is that we desire to demonstrate. And the "truth," to me, is something above and beyond the letter of the truth. When we are knowing the truth, we are living the truth.

We think, and mind creates what we think; but if we do not have that feeling, if we do not have that action, that living that is going on, what good is anything or anyone in our life?

Just briefly, to bring in our principle, I want to state that we are dealing with the Science of Mind, that what we think consciously goes into subconscious mind, and mind begins instantly to create the form, experience, and everything that corresponds with what we consciously think.

In recognizing that there is power in thought, we can use our thought to cause mind to create something that is not already in our experience. We say that there is power in thought. But is there a greater power than our thought? I say there is. I say there is a greater power than thought and

126

that greater power is our self. That greater power is this Presence, or this feeling, that we call God.

Now, in using the letter of truth to get something, we are automatically creating, in our consciousness, a sense of anxiety and a sense of uncertainty, which go into subconscious mind; and mind then creates the experience of that uncertainty, or of that doubt, or of that anxiety.

Let me put it this way. A woman came to me recently and said that she had accepted this science, Science of Mind, to demonstrate the right mate. Fantastic? And into her life came this man. Okay? So now she's got her demonstration.

The only thing is that as soon as she fell in love, she said, this man was the center of her life, and the moment he was the center of her life, she began having one problem after another. She then found she had to be what he wanted her to be. She found herself doing things she didn't want to do and she did them because he wanted her to do them; and she had to do them if he were to stay in her life. And so she began backing off, because she didn't like that experience. She released him, and she began doing her own thing and being herself. Then something very interesting began to happen. The moment she backed off and released him, he became attentive and loving and he began doing everything he could to please her. Fantastic? As soon as he began doing that, she said, "Oh, my God, here he is, this is it!"

And so again she made him the center of her thought and her attention, and he then began going in the opposite direction, and she had to pursue him, woo him, and, again, he was a pain.

And what did she do? She said, "I've got to get back to principle." So she released him and went back to using her thought to be aware of who and what she is, living out of her self. Again, back he came, following her around, doing whatever he could to make her happy, and so forth. Now, it seems that only when she released him and was herself did she have this feeling of completeness, of creative experience with him. But when he became the center of her thought and attention, he demanded—and she had to give—and she was no longer happy. She had this frustration, this pain, this anxiety, and so forth. It was like playing ping pong, you know, going in this direction, that direction, back and forth.

And what's the answer? The answer is that we use our thought to demonstrate the spirit of truth rather than the letter of truth, meaning that we are using this teaching not to get, but to arrive at that feeling of completeness, that feeling of totality that we call God, that we call love. The moment we are expressing love, which has no object, we are free and we have the creative experience. But the moment there is an object in our love, it is no longer love, and we no longer have freedom, we no longer have the creative experience.

We use the letter of truth to demonstrate our good. The moment we demonstrate that good and we forget the principle and we put our attention on person, place, and thing, we've got anxiety and fear. The moment we are trying to get anything, we've got a problem. What I'm getting at is: Arrive at a feeling, arrive at a sense of security, arrive at an experience of simply being your self, rather than using your thought to get anything in any way.

What happens when we are desperately using the Science of Mind to demonstrate our good? We are, in essence, driving our good from us, because we only have what we give and what we are secure about.

I remember years ago when I was in the theater I was invited to read for two parts in the same play. They were both very good but I simply had to have a particular one. And I got the script. I read it, I rehearsed it, I worked over it, I did everything I could, I practically memorized it, and I went in for my reading. Now, what did they do but say, "Okay, we'll read for the part," for the part, you know, that I didn't want, that I didn't care anything about. "We'll read from that one first," they said. They didn't know my feeling about it, but that's what they had me read for first. So I read it. I tossed it off and let it go. And then we got to the excitement of reading for the part that I really wanted and which was going to make me a star.

And so I read it and I was absolutely what? I was absolutely fantastic! I mean, what else?

At any rate, I was called back to read again for the part that I wanted. And once more I was called back to read for the part I wanted. Then I was called back to sign a contract—for the part that I didn't want. It was the part that I only read once, that I wasn't concerned about, and that, you know, I had just tossed off. And that was my demonstration.

I was in the Science of Mind then, not at the level or the way I am now, but I learned something: What we desperately go after, what we desperately desire, what we really want to have—we will never really get; and what we are indifferent about, what we are carefree about—comes into our experience easily. It's there without any sweat or strain.

There's a principle involved in that approach. And so much of treatment is used for the purpose of desperately trying to make something happen. There's got to be, to me, a divine indifference about what we are going to get. It's got to be a divine indifference about whether we are healed or not. There has to be a divine indifference about our demonstration, whatever it is; because if there is not, there is going to be worry, anxiety, and fear in the treatment— in the way that we treat. "I've got to have it! I've got to demonstrate this good!"

Now, the individuals who are overly sensitive, the individuals who are worried and anxious, are what? They are individuals who are trying to get something, who have *got* to get something, who have *got* to make their demonstration—even though they are using the Science of Mind. And this is the point that I am making: In using the Science of Mind, we are automatically directing into mind the worry and the anxiety and the fear that go with using the Science of Mind. Does that make sense?

You might be asking, "Oh? Am I in the right place?" You're in the right place.

You might also be asking, "What are you teaching?" What I'm teaching is the science of self-awareness. What I'm teaching is the science of living, not getting. The moment we try to get something we're no longer living. And the moment our attention is centered on some *one* or some *thing,* we are no longer living.

Now, if our attention, if our purpose, is to center our thought on someone, we've got the problem—because we are taking ourselves away from living, from being, from fulfilling our reason for being, which is to express and reveal our total self. God is not a thing. God is not a person in our life. God is the expression, the action, the feeling of completeness, that you and I are releasing into every moment.

The spirit of the truth then is the recognition that "I am already complete," that "I am God individualized." It is this *feeling*—this feeling that "there is nothing that I cannot do," this feeling of "this power within me." And when I have that feeling, I've got everything. When I've got that feeling, I am in action expressing that identity, that idea, that I call God. But the moment I try to *get* anything, I've lost out, I've lost the feeling, I'm going in the wrong direction. And, yes, I know that the Science of Mind says that

I can have anything that I want. And, yes, I know that the Science of Mind says I must use my thought in a certain way and I'll demonstrate perfect body, money, a job, the right mate, and so on.

But what good is it in having the right mate if I've lost my self, if I don't know who and what I am, if I am not living out of my completeness and out of my self-respect and out of my self-authority? And what good is having money if I'm not happy in what I'm doing? And what good is having the right job if I'm not happy in that job, and if I'm not using my potential and my inner talents in ever-growing and expanding ways?

My goal is always the spirit of truth. It is my self. It is the idea of experience of God as me. And only when I can move out into the world and simply act, be, express, and therefore be divinely indifferent about what is going to happen and be divinely indifferent about what other people think about me and what I'm doing, can I really give, create, express and do, and reveal the genius that resides within my *self*.

Now, who am I talking about? I'm talking about you— this "I" that is in each and every one of us which is only in action when we are no longer trying to get, when we have this carefree, indifferent attitude, or state of mind, about what is going to happen. Okay?

What do I do if I have been given a medical verdict of, let's say, some inconsequential, piddling disease such as cancer? What do I do if I have been told by the doctor that I have cancer?

First of all, I become frantic. Right? I become filled with dread. I remember all the people I know who have died with cancer. And therefore I begin to feel sorry for myself, and I think of all kinds of horrible things in escaping from this particular destiny. But if I am to use this science of self-awareness, I've got to be completely indifferent about whether I live or die. Does that make sense? I've got to be completely indifferent about whether I live or die.

You might be thinking, "My God, what is this man saying?"

I'm saying that if I am indifferent about what is going to happen, I can begin to live. Then I can begin to feel this sense of something within myself that is already there. But I will not have it, I will not touch it, when there is any trace of concern or anxiety that I've *got* to be healed.

In saying that I've *got* to be healed, what am I saying? How am I directing mind, except at the level of "I am incomplete, I am sick, I've got a problem"? That desperation gets in the way of my good, and so I desperately treat to be healed. What happens? I get progressively worse. Or, yes, maybe something begins to happen because I *will* mind to create. But I can't use will power forever. At the moment I take will power away, I demonstrate some kind of physical limitation all over again.

I think, particularly with cancer, we've got to work for the realization of the idea that God is all there is and be divinely indifferent about what's going to happen, because it seems that cancer has a connotation in the consciousness of the world that is absolutely dreadful. And I saw the reaction of many of you out there when I even said the word cancer, you know, when I remarked about something as piddling and inconsequential as cancer. I got all kinds of reactions, indicating that it wasn't inconsequential or piddling at all.

I can use my thought, the letter of the truth, to arrive at the truth. But the truth is that I already am a star. The truth is that I already am a genius. The truth is that I already am complete, and my treatment to get anything denies that completeness. My treatment to demonstrate the right mate, the right job, everything, denies that my good already is. Am I making any sense to anybody? Okay.

So, yes, the Science of Mind says I can have anything I want and I can use the letter of truth to demonstrate that good. But it's only temporary good. Because the law of my being is always in action. And I always have that which I am, that which represents my self. And so it is this *feeling* that is my demonstration. This feeling of joy, this feeling of love, this feeling of excitement, this feeling of enthusiasm, this feeling of completeness—this is God, as me. And when I've got that feeling, I can have a creative relationship with whoever is in my life, because now I'm not begging, now I'm not beseeching, now I'm not wooing, now I'm not pursuing; I'm simply being myself. And therefore as I release person, place, and thing, and I am this beingness, this feeling of God as me, the world then pursues me. Then the law of attraction brings to me that which I am. And now I've got a creative relationship.

A creative relationship has no object. Now, doesn't that sound ridiculous? But it's not ridiculous. It's the truth. Yes, the law of my being always becomes form, and in my experience are those people who help me experience myself, who represent my being, who receive what I am giving. But the moment I make them the object, I'm no longer being, I'm no longer giving, I'm trying to get, and therefore I'm like a yo-yo going back and forth.

Have we ever felt at any time sort of sensitive, on the verge of tears, discouraged, depressed, or something like that? Nobody? Okay. If we have, that's a result of our making someone the object of our thought, centering our attention on getting, demanding, wanting, desiring, needing. I say—now, this doesn't sound very romantic—that the people who are in our experience are the symptoms of our self. I know it is not very romantic to look into somebody else's eyes and say, "Hello, you symptom, you." But that's what they are. The people in our lives are the symptoms of our self.

Does smoking cause cancer? What causes smoking? Smoking is a symptom of an identity. Drinking is a symptom of an identity. Taking drugs is a symptom of an identity. Overeating is a symptom of an identity. Oversex is a symptom of an identity. You know, they call it nymphomania. Nymphomania is something that's out of balance. But it's a symptom, it's not a cause. It's a symptom of reflection of an identity. Okay, now, as we are continually treating to get, trying to add person, place, and thing to our self, we develop these symptoms of trying to get.

Is jealousy love? Anybody here ever been jealous? Well, jealousy is not love in any way whatsoever. In fact, it's the exact opposite. Jealousy is complete insecurity. It's a taking, getting thing. It's not love at all. So, if we are having the symptom of jealousy, it says something about "I," myself. So I can't do anything about the person out there. In order to be free in this experience of God as me, I've got to arrive at this level of self-awareness where I release person, place, and thing, and live and express out of that completeness that God already is as me. But the moment I'm making a demand upon anyone in any way whatsoever, I've got a problem. And it's a symptom of my being outside of God.

What do I mean by being outside of God? This afternoon I asked this question: "Is God a loving, caring God?"

God doesn't care. I mean, if God cared about what happens to other people It wouldn't be God. It would be saying there is a possibility of tragedy, a possibility of negativity. And God doesn't know what negativity is. God doesn't know what incompleteness is. God doesn't know what starvation is. God doesn't know what poverty is. God doesn't know what a problem is. God only knows what

God is. It can only be aware of Itself. And so, those who are outside of God, separated from God, are those who are trying to *get*, those who are even using their thought in trying to get, those who are thinking about themselves in a limited way. And those who are in God are at one with that completeness that already is, and they are not trying to get, in any way whatsoever.

If God were aware of limitation, that awareness of limitation would have destroyed God and It wouldn't be God.

Any time anybody has a pain they're outside of God. They are not aware of who and what they are. They're trying to get, in some way. They are using the letter of truth in order to get something, and that's why they've got the pain. Whenever we try to add to ourselves, we have a conflict within consciousness which manifests as pain.

So, yes, you can treat for things. Yes, you can ask for the right mate. You can ask God for anything. But will God give it to you? God doesn't hear a question. God doesn't hear anyone who begs. God doesn't hear anyone who beseeches. Because that's a denial that good already is.

I simply know who and what I am. The spirit of truth is knowing the truth, living the truth, feeling the truth, being the truth; and mind automatically causes everything out here to correspond with what we are being, what we are living, and what we are expressing. So our attention cannot be on a person—of how I want him or her to behave or what I want from him or her. It's got to be on knowing who and what I am. It's got to be for the purpose of arriving at this feeling of enthusiasm, which is love; at this central completeness, which is love—that asks nothing of anyone. This joy of being myself, God as me—that's love. That's the spirit of truth.

And the letter of truth, yes, can bring us there but it's not the reality. A treatment is a step along the way.

What if you say at the end of every treatment, "Here,

this is the beginning, because it's the beginning now of unfoldment of expression of action of my living that idea that I've identified myself with, and as I live it, as I express it, the things are automatic''? Okay? The letter of truth says that I can give the most fantastic, beautiful treatment, with the right words, in right sequence; I can have the seven steps, or the twenty-five steps, or the forty-five steps, all in proper sequence—and will I demonstrate my good when I arrive at step forty-five? I won't. I'll be so concerned with the steps that I have not touched the spirit of the truth.

One time in New Jersey I had a student in my third year class who always had demonstrations and who always had results. And she gave the worst treatment you could possibly imagine. She couldn't even speak English. It was grammatically incorrect, but it had feeling. It touched something within herself. It touched that feeling, and that feeling acted upon mind, and she had results.

I'm not interested in any step but one. And I say there's only one step in treatment, and that's "God is all there is." That's all I need to know. And as I arrive at that feeling, at that sense of completeness, at that excitement of being myself, God as me, in this joy of living this moment, simply for the sake of living this moment, then I've got everything else. And into my life come the right people, the right things, whatever is necessary, whatever represents this joy that I'm living here and now. That's all I need. That's all you need, to be yourself.

I'm saying that you do not need to be improved upon in any way whatsoever. Did you hear me? I'm saying you don't have to be changed in any way whatsoever. You already are complete.

Now, you say, "I've got all these faults, all these things that I'm doing wrong." I'm not talking about that. I'm talking about you, this "I," this joy of being. Forget your mistakes! They don't count. All you've got is you, "I," which is love. Yes, love reaches out. It embraces. But it doesn't demand anything of anyone. It says, "I acknowledge, I see, the completeness that you already are." It says that you are God individualized and nothing else. And so, as I have that feeling, as I sense that totality, that I'm where I need to be, that's my demonstration—this feeling which is love, which is God, which is the spirit of truth, which is knowing the truth, which is living the truth. And mind takes care of everything else.

So you and I are here not to get. You and I are here to be "I-aware"—"I" which is God individualized as you, as me. Within your being right here and right now already is all you will ever need, all you can ever use. Acknowledge it, be aware of it. It then comes forth into expression, into action, by being this feeling of the spirit of God which is already complete.

Mind, then, reveals to us, not something to *get* but something to give, something to reveal, something to radiate. But in just being ourselves, it is the feeling of completeness. We are automatically radiating this sense of totality, this sense of completeness, and mind takes care of everything else. And out of that feeling, I know that I am in my right and ideal world. Out of that feeling, I know that I have the right people, the right things, all that represent this greatness, this magnificence, this genius that God forever is in action as me.

But it is what I'm feeling *now* that counts. It is what I am expressing *now* that is directing mind. Now is all there is, but in the now is "I," the spirit of truth, the feeling, the totality, the completeness of God as me, as you, in expression, right here, right now.

And so beginneth the lesson.

Dr. Tom Johnson is currently the minister of the West Valley Church of Religious Science, Canoga Park, California. He was previously the minister of the Church of Religious Science in Morristown, New Jersey.

In addition to his work as a minister, which encompasses 13 years, Dr. Johnson is a member of the Board of Directors of RSI, having served in that capacity for 10 years. All of Dr. Johnson's ministerial training was taken in New York City with Dr. Raymond Charles Barker.

Dr. Johnson is a prolific New Thought author, and his works are well known. His published books and other writings include "You Are Always Your Own Experience," "To Love or To Be Loved," "The Power of Surrender," "Your Creative Self," "Your Healing is Today," and "Heaven is an Action—Not a Place."

Dr. Johnson gave his talk, "The Letter of Truth," on March 14, 1979, at his church in Canoga Park, California.

CHAPTER THIRTEEN

Except the Lord build the house,
they labour in vain that build it.
                    —Psalm 127:1

Living on Center

Dr. Raymond K. Lilley

Whether one would talk about living on center, or from center, or from within center, or of the variations which would be adequate and appropriate, really doesn't change the essence of that which we are about to share together.

This morning we want to address ourselves to the realization that there is That within us, there is That which surrounds and sustains us, which merits our attention supremely. It merits our attention uniquely, fully, and wholly. It does not always receive this from us.

Living on center is important. Recognizing the existence of a centeredness in life is important. It tells us that we are acknowledging that significance which all of mankind across the vast history of our existence has insisted upon: The greater than ourselves. The human race in the course of its history has mirrored the need for a knowledge, or at least the credibility, of the existence of something that is greater than itself. Something within the human being says, "Wow, I'm wonderful but if there's not something more than the wonderful me, if there's not something that really comprises the true essence of wonderful me, what am I? I don't know for sure about my continuity. I suspect that there should be something valid about my continuity. But I know nothing of the nature of my human self that can guarantee that I am of continuity. Therefore, if there is to be any hope for a sense of continuum, it must rest in That which is greater than myself.''

Across the ages man has characterized this "greater than" in many ways, for many purposes, in many times. We have not always remembered the credibility of the continuity of things. We have not always mirrored the maturity with which to view the fact that we have been facilitating our existence wherever we were.

We facilitate our existence everywhere in life. We do it under all kinds of circumstances. Someone goes to the kitchen and prepares to make something. Perhaps certain necessary ingredients are not available in the cupboard. It is not possible to get the supplies and get them back in time. You change your mind. You modify. You alter. Sometimes you try to make one ingredient serve for another. Sometimes it serves and sometimes it doesn't. And sometimes you learn that when you try to make do with what is less than what is adequate, it's a little risky and you can't quite pull it off. And so we learn as times goes by.

This happened in the religion of man. It happened in the philosophy of man. It happened in the academia of mankind. And yet we seem to be not yet fully able to understand the reality of a step as a step. Frequently we seem compelled to call the step the journey. The step has to be the total of achievement. We know better. We know that a journey of a mile is not made in one giant step. It's made with many steps. There may be many giant steps insofar as the relative world is concerned, perhaps, with respect to my normal approach to life, or your normal approach to life.

I may extend myself. I may step out and lengthen my stride. I may exert myself to invest that journey with greater vigor than I have ever applied to my endeavors before, and to me it's a giant step. But there may be some behind me or some beside me who stride far more broadly than I and far more rapidly than I. Yet, they may be utilizing a mere portion of their personal potential.

And so we cannot say what that is which is adequate in one total swoop of the thing. We can only say that we understand the progressive unfoldment of life through creation, of which we are a part.

Living on center, therefore, is a matter of keeping our minds focused on the realization that there is that transcendent self which is yet more eminent. It pervades Its creation to the fullest of Its nature. We are hard-pressed to understand this. Today in the modern insights into life that we have, we look at the ancients. We talk about pagans, we talk about crudeness, we talk about the primitive and the uncivilized—and we do all this without ever stopping to think of how pagan and how crude and how uncivilized we shall appear perhaps just 1,000 years hence.

If you want to do an experiment in what it might be like, in a very miniscule measure, just go back in your closet or your little trunk, or wherever it is that you have it, and dig out your high school annual and take a look at yourself. See what they wore at the time you were in school. And you don't have to be too old to do that. In 10 years, in 8 years, look at the hair style difference and the clothing difference. "That's me? My, I was young and puny!" And at that time you thought you were what? Ageless and mighty and wise. So you were—to the extent of your ability to receive it.

And this is why we are reminding ourselves that there is a center from which to express, because wherever we are and whoever we are and whatever we're doing, from the mightiest achievement of our spiritual perception and our intellectual acumen and our physical prowess, there is always yet more.

The Finns have a word for that. I think it's "susi." It means "there is more yet." I've had a lot of Finns interpret that for me, and they put a lot of secular meaning in it, and I accept that. But it has a deep, spiritual meaning. It's a word they say to themselves when they're confronted with something. When you look at a situation you can say to yourself, "Lo and behold, with all of the grandeur, with all of the limitation, with all of the frustration, with all of whatever, there is more yet to be." We remind ourselves of this.

That's living on center. It's living with the sense of a transcendent intelligence that wants to elevate us. This is what Jesus meant, to my mind.

I've been checking up on myself and I did again this morning. I have been just as prone to say, as many have, "Jesus said" and "Jesus meant." Well, I really don't know, in all honesty I don't know what he meant. I know what the things he said mean to me. So what I'd like to say this morning is that this is what I think Jesus meant when he was saying it, or what it meant to me, because nobody really knows what Jesus said or meant except Jesus. But to me, what he appeared to mean when he said, "Your Father hath knowledge of all that you need before you ask," is: "And above and beyond that, that you can either ask or think, beyond that, putting it to shame, in essence, has God prepared for those that love Him, if we will but receive it." Maybe he didn't mean it in exactly that way, but that's what it meant to me.

There is that in life that awaits the opportunity to gush forth. It's like an artesian well under the geological structure of the earth, kept down only by the weight and the mass and the contour of the geology of the earth. Sometimes just pitting a little hole down in the earth fifty feet will release a column of water high in the air because of the natural pressure. It has always been there. And over a period of time, with the oscillating and the movement of the earth, it might even find its way to the surface through a little fissure and become a trickle and finally a bubbling spring. But in the absence of having achieved that through the span of time, it's there to pop forth.

Life is at the center of each of us waiting release into action. It wants to be the best of whatever it is that we want it to be, if that is in conformity with truth. Life won't restrain us from anything. What we teach in Religious Science is that we can have anything we want as long as it's not at the expense of another's dignity. But we forget that last part sometimes.

Remembering whether or not this which I desire at this moment impinges upon the dignity of another is an act of honesty and integrity. It's an act to which we ought to address ourselves more frequently. And by living from center we can do this.

What is one of the ways that will help us to arrive at this point? One of the ways that I have found useful is to begin with myself and say to myself, "Raymond, what are you worth? And I have learned over a period of time to say to myself with a modicum of humor and of sadness at the same time, "Sometimes not so much as you think you are, and a lot of the time much more than you dare to think you are."

And it is in that context that I say to myself, "Now, where is your problem? Why don't you dare to think that you are more than you've allowed yourself to think? And what is it that causes you to be so audacious as to think that you are more than you really are?" And these are questions worthy of asking. They are questions that bear down upon us. But so frequently we don't like to face these questions because we like to deal in the outer.

Oh, it is so much more fun to deal in the outer. "If we can just push that person around, and just nick that person into action, and just put the brakes on for the other person." It's much more fun to do it that way. Or is it? I really don't think so.

Let us look at some of the idioms of our language and see how ridiculous we frequently make ourselves in our own eyes, much less somebody else's. For years I've been reading in many publications the astute perceptions of individuals who are endeavoring to contribute to the fiber of strength in the human race. They have risen above the general, traditional, heavy negativism of being worthless worms of the dust. It's not too far above us, however, when you look at it in its particular perspective. The aphorism is this: "Behold, man, I'd like to tell you a little bit about you and about me; you, with your limited, squeezed up concept of God that you think did everything. There's a great big world out there, fella, and that great big world is the result of more than your little God. That world is the result of something vast. In fact, that world is so vast that we know there are more worlds like ours. Don't you know that there may even be worlds out there with people in them or creatures in them who are more advanced than we are?" I have just made an observation that puts us where we belong. But what do we do about it? Let's look at what we do about it.

We have this great intellectual, perceptive insight that there's more in this universe than our own world, more than our solar system, more creatures than us, and they may be better than we are—but what do we do with the knowledge of the laws of our world that we have? Do we use those laws assiduously to advance our inquiry and investigation into the nature of that which might have made that thing out there that's bigger than we are? Or do we do it to fill our pocketbooks? Do we do it to keep the headaches away from us? Do we do it to keep everybody our friends? How do we use this insight that there is a greatness that may be so great that it has worlds that are bigger and vaster than ours?

We make fools of ourselves when in one breath we say, "My cosmology includes the concept that a kind of intelligence has created something fabulous. The cosmology is in the palm of my hand. I speak the word and I always have a parking place. I speak the word and I never get a headache. I speak the word and everybody is my friend." What in heaven's name kind of garbage is *that*?

You know, I have nothing against finding a parking place. I have nothing against getting rid of a headache. I have nothing against being prosperous. I have nothing against being happy. But I think the time is ripe among us when the prosperity that we seek, when the serenity that we seek, when the friendliness that we seek, should be that which we seek for the purpose of advancing the knowledge of the presence of the kingdom of God within mankind, and not for reminding the world, "Hey, Buster, I'm here and look out, I'm coming down the avenue." And that's all right too, if you have your parade permit. But frequently we don't. We parade our bigoted little egos in the guise of having been sent forth by God. And "by God" means what? We don't always know. We don't always wait to see. We presume out of our meager insight. Why? Because it's very possible that God could have sent *me* here. But I don't want anybody under any delusions. *I* sent me here.

So we say to ourselves, "There is a center from which to live." That center is real.

I once made a statement that I am going to reiterate at this moment. I made a statement that there's no room in this church for minorities. I want to reiterate that statement.

There is no room in this church for a minority. You can say, "Well, what's that got to do with living on center?" Everything. How can you live a life that says there is one God, one Life, one Presence, one Intelligence, one Love, one Everything, and then think of yourself or someone else as a minority? Our world is sick with people who are fractured in their thinking. Jesus said, "In the world ye have tribulation but be of good cheer, I have overcome the world." In the world you have minorities, you have schisms, you have poverty, you have every kind of thing to which one could lay one's tongue. The message of Religious Science, to me, is that we live in Mind and we live in the purity of consciousness.

In consciousness there are no heavy taxes. In consciousness there is no limitation. In consciousness there is no inflation, there are no minorities, there are no lesser or greater. There are only *we* who are of the God of all people.

I stand here this morning to announce to each of you— member or visitor—that I challenge you to rise into the consciousness that would fill this place with people of this likemindedness that we might go forth and say to the world, "We're tired of taking the title you stamped upon our back."

Have you ever been to parties where the fun of the party is that some joker writes a sign saying, "kiss me," and puts it on the back of the most bashful guy in the office? Everyone at the Christmas party runs around kissing this bashful person who doesn't know what to do and doesn't know why they're doing it; he never kissed anybody in the office in his life. Finally somebody pulls the tag off and says, "Well, you say, 'kiss me.'" And he says, "No, I didn't, somebody did that to me."

I'm saying, "Let's take that somebody's tag off our back. Let's start to live from center. Let's start to live in the belief that there's only one life, that the color of a skin, that the tone of a language, that the twang or whatever it is, doesn't change that oneness. Let's prove to ourselves that we are one in truth and in fact, by living in the knowledge that when we meet someone it's no different than if I meet a person who's wearing a red dress or a white dress. How can I help knowing one dress is red and one is white save I be color blind? Therefore, if I meet a fair-skinned person or a dark-skinned person, I will know it. But in my consciousness there can be no more difference about the skin than there can be about the dress or the color of the suit or a tie or no tie. And until we start living *that* way and stop trying to solve our problems by little nicknames that we've assigned, to the denigration of our spiritual stature, we are going to suffer, and we deserve it. But not in this church, I hope to God. I hope we will live in that consciousness of on-centeredness in which we are all one, and in which we make the other person responsible for living with their limitation but which we will refuse to descend to. We must *know* that this is a place of the fullness of life, where every man, woman, and child is responsible for himself or herself and is free to experience the dignity of personage in God.

Centered living will solve so many of our social problems. There are no wealthy persons who could hang on to excess wealth, in the face of starving peoples, if they live on center. You don't have to be badgered for taxes and assessments, and you don't need ministerial tirades to pry out of your pocketbook excess monies to help people. If you're living on center, it's flowing through you. It should be flowing through you. And if it's not flowing through me, I am not living on center.

We had two weeks of glorious vacation, of mingling with the variety of the beautiful people of America. And my heart saddens when I think how we've let ourselves be blinded to our mutual beauty. We have a principle to live. There's no better place in this city to start living it than in the First Church of Religious Science of Palo Alto, where we believe there is one Life, one Mind, one Presence, one Power, and one Person—God in each *equally*—and where we believe in working together to help each other where we may not be accepting the principle equally. The call is to you.

Dr. Raymond K. Lilley is pastor of the First Church of Religious Science of Palo Alto, California. Previously he was pastor of the Salem, Oregon church.

Previous to completion of his studies in Religious Science, Dr. Lilley had extensive studies at the Unity School of Christianity.

Dr. Lilley is a former member of the Board of Education of RSI, and he is currently serving on the Board of Directors.

He authored a booklet, "Take Time to Think," plus various articles on Religious Science, New Thought, and Eastern Religions.

The talk, "Living on Center," was presented by Dr. Lilley at the Palo Alto church on July 9, 1978.

CHAPTER FOURTEEN

Our only goal is to fully express Spirit in every area of consciousness.

—Little

New Thought About the Mystery of Longevity
Reverend Bill Little

Today I want to tell you about a sort of mystery, a mystery that has been going on for about ten years in scientific circles. And it has, in a sense, broadened into metaphysical circles; it has come out of the physical sciences into the metaphysical. It's a mystery that is receiving a lot of publicity. It has to do with longevity, living a long, fruitful life.

Today we are investigating things on the basis of: What causes old age? Why do people die?

This is not totally new. It's not a field that came about last year or the year before. People have been doing investigations on that for quite a while. But today it's in the forefront.

I'd like to tell you a little bit about the background that I see in it and connect it with consciousness and what we're doing with our conscious mind, and then we'll see if we can come to something as grandiose as the secret to life.

Several years ago I was working in Atlanta doing some research at Georgia Tech, and one of the professors who was there, Dr. Gus Stanford, was doing a kind of research, different from mine, that was fascinating to me. He was doing research on memory—the transfer of memory from one animal to another. He trained a group of rats, as usual, and in a maze.

He would cause the early demise of rats and inject various parts of their anatomy into some mice to see if there was any transfer of the memory. And, of course, he did get a transfer. He got a very marked transfer in the capability of the mice. The first time they were put into the maze, they knew exactly how to go through it. This happened over and over again.

He did some auxiliary experiments with it and found that the transfer of memory going on between the two types of animal did not have anything to do, strangely enough, with chemicals. It wasn't a matter of the chemistry of the various things that were being injected. You could change the chemical structure; it wasn't that. It had to do with the magnetic fields that were involved in this substance that was transferred.

He found that if he took this substance and first subjected it to a magnetic field he could destroy the memory, and the memory wouldn't be transferred to the mice.

You might say, "Well, what has this got to do with metaphysical thought?"

Today we know from many teachings, eastern as well as western, biofeedback as well as meditation, that the human body is not just what we've thought it was all along. The human body has some aspects to it that make it seem very much like an energy system. Whether we're controlling the functions of the body through biofeedback mechanisms or we're measuring the outputs of the body while people are in meditation—whatever way we're looking at it—we're seeing the body as a very delicate energy system. And this is good, because what we're seeing basically is that the nervous system which, of course, covers the entire physical body and transfers nervous energy from one part of the body to

another is causing definite changes in the cell structure of
the body. The nervous system is an electrical system, it's a
wiring system, so to speak. We're beginning to understand
that all cells everywhere—muscle cells, bone cells, all sorts
of organ cells—are very receptive to the energies going
through the nervous system.

I said earlier that the memory transfer that was observed
in Dr. Stanford's experiments had to do with magnetic
fields. Today we can update this kind of information and
we can see that the energy which flows through our nervous
system is literally creating an electric and a magnetic field.
Our nervous system is a live wire, it's an electrical impulse
flying down some sort of tissue, and an electric and magnetic field is being transferred, as there are nerve impulses
going through us all the time. These magnetic fields, it's
thought, are literally creating in cells that surround the
nervous system—including the muscle cells, all the tissues
of the body—imprints. They are literally transferring a sense
of memory to these cells, so that today we think the entire
body is some sort of memory center. We remember things
with our whole physical structure. In computers I guess you
would call it the memory bank.

To metaphysicians, this is not such a new thing. Years
ago we knew that if a person came to a spiritual practitioner
to get rid of scars from an operation or a fall or something
like that, what had to be dealt with was the emotional
memory that the person still stored about the operation or
the fall. That emotional memory needed, in a sense, to be
erased. The memory cells, which in this case were the actual
physical cells, needed to lose their memorized pattern of
behavior which came because at the instant of the operation,
perhaps, or the accident, a nervous impulse transmitted
itself through the nervous system, radiated its field, and
produced a very definite change in the lifestyle of those
cells. And we call it a scar. Erase the emotional memory

and you erase the scar. So metaphysicians were aware of this a long time ago. Now, you know, science as usual is catching up, and it's doing a very beautiful job of investigating this.

So I want to take you one step further. I want to take you into a field now that has not been investigated yet, a field that is still kind of on the forefront, on the fringes, of this. I want to get back to what I started with, and that was the idea of longevity. "Why do we grow old and die?" I think what's going to happen is that the answer to this will be found in memory.

Human cells are very interesting things. When you study them physiologically and biologically, you find out that they have two basic ways of operating. Cells do repetitive things very well. The heart cells, for example, go through a certain kind of motion. The muscle cells in the walls of the heart go through a certain kind of motion repetitively. It doesn't take any great intelligence to do this, it's just that they're well-designed to repeat that motion again and again. That's one kind of operation cells go into, a repetitive operation, over and over, it's not complex. They do it once, it's done. They do it another time, it's done. They're good at that.

And then there's this second function of cells which we're only coming to understand now, and that function is to accumulate memory. The first function is not a tremendous stress on the life of the cell. If you've got a heart cell or a muscle cell on the tissue of the heart, it can perform that beating motion over and over again without accumulating tremendous stress. It stretches, let's say, at one time, and then it relaxes, and between each movement there's a relaxation period so that, in a sense, the stress is released totally and the cell returns to its original form, and there's no problem.

But the memory application of the cell is totally different.

When cells accumulate memory, it's just what we say; it's cumulative. It keeps building up and up and up. The electromagnetic signals that go through the nervous system keep making impressions upon the cells over and over again so that, in a sense, the whole body—almost like a magnetic tape—is getting reimpressed, all the time, reimpressed with more and more impressions that come from the activities of our life, emotions that happen when we see certain people—all of these impressions going on to the cells again and again and again. So it's a cumulative action for the cells.

I suspect what we're going to find out is that the tissue cells of the human body can only take so much accumulation of memory. It takes a lot of energy for a cell to remember to act in exactly the right way which is appropriate for a person who has lived for, say, 40 years, with all these events, with all these memories stored in the nervous system and in the cells. The cell has, shall we say, a "responsibility" to act in a certain way which portrays 40 years worth of impressions. And that kind of memory stored in the cell itself takes an awful lot of the cell's energy, a cumulative form of memory.

It doesn't take much for the cell to do its basic job—let's say, beat the heart—but suppose the nervous system of the person has been exposed to lots of shocks, emotional shocks, shocks that come from dealing with people, shocks from business failures, on and on; then the cells of the heart have not only got their original intention, their original job, but they've got years and years worth of memory to cope with.

Well, I think it's very simple. We degenerate in our physical bodies anyway, degenerate and die, because the memory load gets too high. The cells simply can't remember that much. It takes too much of their living energy, and so physical structures pass away. In a sense, you might say, death then is simply dropping off what really is now obsolete and no longer of any use so that the individual has a fresh start.

In a sense, you can look at the physical body as a storage mechanism of the impressions that have come along all through the years stored as memory.

In the church office we have a couple of techniques of erasing and redoing tape recordings. I bring this up because I think there is some connection between the simple device that we call a tape recorder and what's happening here in the electromagnetic systems of our bodies. You can take something called a bulk tape eraser, which is just a device which puts out a varying magnetic field—very much like what Dr. Stanford used at Georgia Tech—and put it on a tape, move it around a little bit, switch on the controls, and before you know it the tape is erased and ready to go again. The memory has been destroyed. The memory is eliminated, the tape is in a state so that new impressions can be made and the impressions will be very clear.

There's another way we can do it. We can take the same tape and put it on a tape recorder and record something new, and the old memory disappears. Sometimes there's a crossover in that method. Sometimes you get what's called "cross-talk." The old memory and the new recording sort of blend with each other, so obviously it's best for us to do the erasing mechanism.

And, you know, I think that consciousness has a great analogy to this. Down through the ages, especially in the east, we've been taught that meditation is a healthy thing to do, and they mean it in the sense of *healthy*. It enables the body to experience physical health. People have said that when you meditate regularly you'll find lots of things changing in the body. You'll find that especially old problems, old wounds, so to speak—oh, you know, someone broke a leg years ago and it's never really healed right; an organ that hasn't functioned well in many years—you'll find these things being healed very quickly with meditation techniques.

Well, what's going on in meditation? The consciousness is exposed to the vastness of the infinite. In a sense, the nervous system at that time is functioning in a certain way. It's functioning in a way that resembles a bulk tape eraser. The nervous system is transmitting electromagnetic energy to all the cells of the body in such a way as to get rid of the impressions of memory that have happened maybe many, many times—very strong, very powerful impressions—and they're erased. The nervous system transmits energies which are very similar to varying magnetic fields at that point. The consciousness of the individual is aware in a pure state —not unaware in a chaotic state thinking about things, thinking about personality roles, thinking about all these relative situations in life.

In meditation the consciousness is in a pure state, a vast unbounded state. And at that point the nervous system responds with a certain hum, you might say. It vibrates at a certain level and essentially erases perhaps even years and years of experiences from the memory cells; and they're ready to go again, ready to be new.

When I think of these kinds of scientific analogies I always think of the Christian teachings, because so much in Christianity speaks to scientists. Jesus put this all in a very nice nutshell when he said, "Ye must be born again." Nicodemus didn't understand the comment, of course. He was puzzled by it. He thought he had to reenter his mother's womb, and so forth. And Jesus pointed out that Nicodemus was really dumb to think like that. "Ye must be born again." In essence, he said, "You're a teacher, you're a rabbi, you've gone through all the teachings," meaning, "You know about meditation. Why can't you understand what it does?" And so he spoke to him in such a way as to convey the idea that it is necessary for the human individual to experience, shall we say, a starting point, an initial point, a blank start. It is necessary for us to regularly immerse ourselves in an infinite consciousness so that the memories, the stored emotional mental memories of years and years, essentially can be drained.

There's a very interesting passage—this is not unique in the New Testament with Jesus, it was also talked about quite a bit in the Old Testament—in the Book of Ecclesiastes, Chapter 3. The whole chapter is quite interesting in terms of energy and our use of energy. But one particular paragraph points to that.

See if you can pick up a poetic way of expressing just exactly what we've been talking about. Now, this is thousands of years ago. "That which hath been is now." If that's not a description of memory, I don't know what is. And, "That which is to be hath already been." A description of how memory propagates itself, because the individual has no choice but to allow the memory stored within to develop into thought and feeling and produce results similar to what has happened. And, "God requireth that which is passed." In other words, "Get erased." The universe requires the stored up energies of the past. It requires the draining of the emotional hot spots. It requires all the hurts, all the resentments, all the traumas, all the fears of the past. God wants them, because God can't be new as an individual until the memory structure, the physiological, the neurological memory structure, has a sense of being cleansed.

There is a second way in which we can experience erasure of the old memory. The second way is unique to human consciousness; and it is not a real analogy with any kind of mechanical or electrical device. It has to do with the sense of spontaneously conscious individuals, individuals who are capable of being made new through being aware of what they are. And it works something like this: It's as if each one of us has around us a mental, emotional shell, which for most people is quite transparent. We have certain emotional boundaries that we don't go beyond, feelings with certain people that keep our conversation along specific lines. We also have feelings about the world and the situations of the outer and the places we work and the houses and the areas we live in, which make sure that we travel along certain lines. We have thought or belief systems which keep us associated with certain organizations, and so forth. We have these transparent shells which, in a sense, form our personality. When people, through awareness of one simple little center called "I," project themselves into a new dimension, once they do that, they're bursting through a shell, a crystal shell, so to speak, into a new level of activity, and when they do that, they're in a very real sense engaging in the erasure of the memory patterns stored within the physiological system.

For example, let's take a person who's interested in physical healings, and let's say the situation is a chronic disease, for years and years arthritis or heart condition or something like that. He suffered with it, at least initially, eventually went to a doctor to get some sort of medicine which enabled him to persevere in the midst of the situation, and eventually learned how to adapt, so with the arthritis or with the heart condition he could live without too much change, learn to live with it, so to speak. All right, right now let's say the person is here today sharing these ideas and is interested in bursting through the shell.

The first step is to come down to a purely simple sense of "I." The first step is to take the sense of "I" away from what has been. And we do this consciously. We consciously withdraw the sense of "I" from the familiar background, from what doctors have told us, from the experiences we've had—we take it away. We take the sense of "I" alone, by itself. This is the image in the Christian teaching of going into the closet and communing with the Father who is in secret. It's the withdrawal of the conscious awareness into a chamber of secrecy. And the individual at that point is literally in the midst of the miraculous, because at that point it is possible, when we are not associating with what has been—with the memory—to project ourselves into newness. It is possible at that point to image and feel and appreciate ourselves as vital, vibrant health.

People might say, "Oh, you're ignoring reality." Oh, am I? Watch. Reality may be more than what people say it is. The fact that I am is also reality. And I'm using the I am in a very intelligent way at this point. I'm allowing the I am to contemplate itself separate from the facts, separate from the condition, separate from the disease, separate from how I've learned to live with it, and so forth. I am contemplating what I am, with a sense of total freedom, with a sense of joy, with a sense of exuberance, at the vitality and the strength that I am. This works especially well in these chronic conditions because, you know, the chronic conditions are those of the most transparent states. Physical dis-ease that is chronic has been there over and over and over again, and it's really transparent; and we get to the point where we don't even notice it, and we don't even notice the continuous physical pain sometimes.

At that point, the individual sense of "I" is moving away, turning 180 degrees away, coming within, contemplating itself as a new being, a new full expression. This is a projection out of the crystalized shell. It's the conscious mind able to move through the barriers into a new level of being. And only consciously can we do that. The conscious mind is the only instrument that can do that.

What happens? Well, it's the experience of everyone that the moment you break through your familiar dimensions you are going to find that those dimensions have a pull, they have a gravitational pull. They're not so quickly done away with. Suddenly what was a transparent shell of feelings and thoughts and so forth becomes a little bit more opaque and we begin to see it. We begin to see all the little objections, resistances, to newness. We begin to see the memory stored within our inner parts. We begin to see all in us that would prevent us from this newness. It raises its head, and it raises it as certain thoughts and certain moods; it raises it very often as other people and, "Oh, no, dear, you know you can't do that. In your condition, don't even try, sweetheart."

Yes, yesterday makes a valiant attempt to be tomorrow. The shell which was transparent makes a great attempt to become quite dense and opaque and say, "Come on, this is as far as you can go and you know it, now stop."

At that point, what has to happen is the development of spiritual strength within the individual. You see, it's not just enough to know that the conscious mind projects me into newness. It projects me into new life, into a new dimension of being alive. I must also deal with the humanness of me which offers resistances to such newness. And in doing so, I develop the strength of spirituality.

The truth of spirituality is that we are absolutely free to conceive of ourselves in any way we wish to be. But the strength of spirituality is drawing with us our psychology and our physiology into this new realm. And that takes the strength of courage, intelligence, faith, devotion; it takes all of these qualities we hear so much about. They are to be developed in pulling the lagging aspects of our being into the freshness of now.

The memory which is stored within the cells which is cumulative, remember—which builds up—can be changed. It can be erased, so to speak. The memories of old experiences and how "they caused me to feel this way and do that thing" and so forth and so on—all of this can be erased. All of this can be handled. It *does* take us being new. Now, does that mean we have to go out and conquer the world and establish a new large corporation? No, that's not what I'm talking about. I'm saying, you can project yourself to some realm in which you wish to be new, something you have never done before, a way in which you have never considered yourself.

Sit down this afternoon and write down on a pad of paper at least five ways that you have never allowed yourself to consider yourself. You know, if you're around 85, think about the fact that you've never really driven go-carts and that you'd really love to. Or, perhaps, if you're a waitress in a restaurant, think of how you'd love to fly 747s. This is not foolishness. It is a sign of your freedom. You can say, "Oh, no, I couldn't do that. That's ridiculous. That's going too far!" Well, why is it going too far? Because you haven't yet learned how to develop the spiritual strength to take the psychological you and the physical you along with the spiritual you. But you can project.

Once the projection is made, the rest of the job is erasing the memory, erasing the memory stored within the cells, being "born again." You see how it fits very well into the Christian idea of being born again. So what happens at that point?

Well, let's take the person who wants to switch professions from the waitress to the pilot of the 747. What comes up? First of all, no doubt what comes up is a mood. Moods are tricky things, you know. They have no labels on them. They have no forms to them. You can't say it's this emotion or that emotion. Today psychologists know that there's no such thing as a pure emotion. There are mixtures of emotion, sort of a sea of uneasiness, anxiety, we give it all these strange words—trepidation, and so forth. A wet blanket—maybe that's the best expression. What is this thing? Well, it doesn't matter what it is. It's some accumulation of your spleen trying to vibrate again—the memory stored somewhere in the neurological, physiological system. What do you do with it?

One of the things to do is to develop a sense of courage. There is such a thing as spiritual courage. In fact, to be spiritual is a courageous thing, especially in our world today. Spiritual courage means standing up in the midst of the mind without even support of your own thoughts, and saying, "This is where I'm going, this is what I'm doing, this is what I choose; and if my thoughts can't support it, tough, they'll have to change."

Moods are not here to overwhelm any human being. Most people are scared to death of their feelings. Most people won't go near an emotional state. They'll do everything they can to get out of it and let another person cajole them out of it and persuade them about how good they are, and so forth. We'll do anything to get away from our emotional states. We don't have to be subject to emotional states. They are just vibrations of the liver, or of some other thing like that. We're being run by electromagnetic impressions. We shouldn't be.

Moods are not meant to run us. To be able to stand up in the midst of a mood and proclaim order and proclaim peace and say, "There is but one God and that God is consciousness and I am conscious that I am consciousness"— that's spiritual courage.

Then comes the thought, "Oh, but it takes so many years to get the training to fly the 747s!" Now the belief nature begins to come up. "What will I do in between? How will I earn my living?" These are all the things which would love to kill the spirit. There's lots of imagery in the Bible about killing the spirit—Herod killing the firstborn of the Jews.

The firstborn is that which is born first. What's born first in the mind? A sense of spiritual aliveness, a sense of intuitive joy. Herod is that king of the world who slaughters the firstborn. What is Herod? Herod is just us. It's the intellectual us that insists that "we have to be logical about this thing, you know." Again, just a vibration of some part of the memory stored within the cells.

What we don't understand is that it is our responsibility and our privilege to change that. If we don't, we sit here like an accumulator absorbing memories, absorbing experiences, over and over and over again, until the cells can't take it any more, and we go.

Longevity is a matter of insisting on the spiritual consciousness of newness—not being put down by any aspect of the mind which would try to hang on to the past.

So we develop the strength of intelligence. What's happening is that an automatic memory pattern stored somewhere—who cares where—is coming up like the voice of some well-meaning relative, you know, echoing through the ages, saying, "Oh, dear, you know that this takes a long time to do and you've got to feed yourself now." And on and on and on. All of this is automatic memory. It's like someone pushing a tape button and you've got tape number 362 from May 25th, 1947.

As a conscious individual, are you not more important than the tape that is playing from yesterday? Of course you are! So it takes intelligence. It takes the intelligence of perceiving what is really true, not what is emotionally backed by yesterdays. The person who clearly and boldly proclaims that his or her choice to move into this new field produces the opportunities, and produces the right jobs, and produces the right training, and does so efficiently and easily, is using the highest form of intelligence. That person is dissolving yesterday's tapes and yesterday's arguments of limitation and is changing the very cells of the physical structure, sending new messages of freedom down the pathways of the neurological system, electromagnetically implanting energies which will allow even the physical body to function in a more healthy way. This is why people through the ages have said, "A right, healthy, good, prosperous, positive attitude is going to cause the body to be healthy." Of course it is, because the physical body is going to vibrate at the level of the nervous system. So we have the development of spiritual strength at that point.

We're going to find in the next few years that this kind of activity, this throwing one's self ahead, taking the spirit of your being and throwing yourself ahead into challenges that you never dreamed of using, being, and expressing, is a key to health on all levels—mental, emotional, and physical.

There is a very beautiful quote that stuck in my mind some years ago when I was studying a little bit with Eric Butterworth, the Unity Minister, in New York. He said, "Spiritual growth is not a matter of changing yourself as much as it is a matter of being more yourself." At that point he was saying, "Emphasize your ability to project yourself, your being, into a new experience. Don't worry so much about the changes that have to come about. They will come about. First, take care of the business of projecting yourself into the new. Be more yourself. Express more of the fulfillment of your desires. Listen in the heart to the spirit that is within you which says, 'Behold, I make all things new,' and let it announce itself through you."

Sure, the changes will come about, certainly they will. The resistance will crop up. It's going to raise its head, it's going to try to hold you back, all of that will happen. That's part of growth, that's part of developing the spiritual muscles. "But by all means," he says, "project yourself into the new."

Oddly, this is the inner meaning of spiritual teaching through the ages. The background that Jesus came from was the ancient Cabala. The ancient Cabala predates the Old Testament; it was only written down years after the Old Testament, but it was passed down by word of mouth by the Jewish mystics for thousands of years before the Old Testament. If you read that book, you find out that their most potent description of life is that spirit is an energy forever breaking through forms it has made. They used images such as the chicken coming forth from the shell, the plant coming out of the seed.

Spirit is an energy which must have a resistance to it in order to develop the strength to break forth. In fact, the ancient Cabalists used to say, "The resistance to spiritual growth is as important as the growth itself, as the spirit itself." If we don't have that within us, the humanness within us that says, "Wait a minute, not so fast," we don't have the ability to see the spirit alive *through* us. It's a relative situation. We can only tell spirit's movement, its dynamism, by the fact that there's a part of us that says, "Hey, slow down there."

But that doesn't mean we stop. It means that there's a job to be done. It means that there is courage, devotion, faith, intelligence, love—all of these to be developed. That's all it means.

Reverend Bill Little has been a minister in Religious Science for 5 years. He delivered his sermon, "New Thought About The Mystery Of Longevity," on March 11, 1979 at the Monterey, California church, where he has been pastor since 1976.

CHAPTER FIFTEEN

Is there any limit? Is there any end to progress?
Is there any end to this power within us that leads
us to a fuller expression of self and more and
more accomplishment in a positive way in our
continued progression in this thing called life?
No, there is no end to it. No, there is no limit to
it. Therefore, there is no limit to you.

—Neale

How To Be the Person You Want To Be

Reverend Jay Scott Neale

This morning's talk is on an important subject. The category of advancing self is important primarily because many people go through life with ideas of the person they *want* to be. They have concepts, they have dreams, desires, hopes —all these things are going through their mind; and they say, "Well, as soon as I am that person, I'll feel better. As soon as I am that person, I will be happy. As soon as I have wealth"—and on and on. The idea is that you will never be that person unless you know you are that person NOW. You are already the thing you are looking for. This is the wisdom of the ages. The great, the good, the wise, the just, of the ages have expressed to us very clearly that "what you're searching for, you're searching with."

One of the foremost contributors to this teaching, Judge

Thomas Troward, was one of the great legal minds in England. He was a great Judeo-Christian biblical scholar. At one time he was the governor of Punjab, India, and he had an opportunity to explore some of the religions in that particular area. Through his own understanding and his own education, he correlated what the teaching of the east and what the teaching of the west were saying, and he put it into a language that could be understood. And, of course, he made a major contribution to Ernest Holmes' own work. We owe a great deal to Thomas Troward, and that's why we teach him as much as we do.

One of the things that Troward talked about was the idea of how to evolve from secondary causation—letting the world tell you how to feel—to first cause, and allowing yourself to live and move and have your being at a new level of awareness, as you. "I move forward from me to this experience," NOT "from the experience to me." In other words, "I, today, know that I am Infinite Mind in action, Infinite Intelligence in action, and I have all the power I need, all the intelligence I need, all the genius I need, to move forward and solve anything I need to solve, in a positive way."

If you have a problem, it is nothing more than an algebraic equation. At the end of that equation is the answer. All you have to do is pull back and let yourself see a broader perspective of the same concept. If you demonstrate a problem in your life, any good student of this teaching knows it is there for only one reason: it's there for you to solve. It is there because you have made a demand and you are therefore involved in growth; and if you are involved in growth all the time, you need to let go and evolve into the new.

My topic is based on my treatment for Creative Thought Magazine for June, "I am the person I want to be." I want to share this with you and explore it and use it as a foundation for our lesson this morning. I begin the treatment this way: "I now let my thought flow in the realization of God's presence as me, inspiring me to demonstrate more of the Divine nature in everything I do." This is a very important point to understand. The concept is not new. In Romans 12:2 it says, "And be not conformed to this world, but be ye transformed by the renewing of your mind." And then it goes on to give you a reason for doing this: "that ye may prove what is that good and acceptable and perfect will of God." Now, what is this talking about?

A good illustration is the new plastic that has a memory within it. When it establishes a shape it remembers its original shape. If you apply pressure to the plastic, the stress will bend it out of shape, or it will conform to the pressure applied to it, until you do something. The minute you release the pressure, it goes "boing," right back to its natural shape again.

The same thing is true of you and me. We have a natural state of being, a natural way to express ourselves. We are naturally harmonious, naturally healthy, naturally abundant, naturally happy. We are naturally joyful; the purpose of life is to express Itself in a joyful way; life is joy in action. When we let this happen and let our natural state of being unfold as us, we just go from happiness to happiness, from joy to joy. If we have a problem, great! We know there's an answer to it. So we move on. We look at life as an adventure, and we can say, "This is my opportunity to know more about me today. As I become more of a blessing to me, I become more of a blessing to everything around me. Therefore, I let go and let myself grow in this experience. This is a beautiful state of being." If we allow this beautiful state of being to be our awareness, it will manifest as our experience because, people, again, you and I are the cause of every single thing that happens to us—every single thing. There is nothing happening to you in your world that you do not cause.

A lot of people don't like to hear that, and they want to turn and run away from it. Well, remember, what you're running away from you are going to take with you.

To explore this further, how many times have you had a negative experience happen in your world and the first thing you do is say, "I *knew* that was going to happen," and then blame it on somebody else? Or, "I *knew* they would act that way." Well, that's the only way you would let them act. If they acted in another way you'd be wrong; and people will do anything they can to prove they are not wrong.

People will go miles and miles and miles out of their way just to prove that they're right in a negative way! How many people do you know who will get up in the morning and say, "Hey, it is a good day today"? You can always recognize the pessimist, who will answer, "What's good about it?" and then spends the whole day trying to prove it's terrible. A pessimist gets up looking for something terrible to happen, and it does, and then he's satisfied. You can tell they are satisfied by the frown on their face.

Again, we want to explore our own self and find out for ourselves what is happening as ourselves so that we can evolve in a higher and clearer way. We can transform ourselves by the renewing of our mind only by letting go and letting ourselves understand what we already are.

A new thought is important because "Your newest thought," as Dr. Barker says, "may not be your best thought, but it's your newest one, and you should pay attention to it."

The idea is that if you are going along and everything seems to be the same, it's like going down a road in Texas. Did you ever drive in Texas? I was raised in Texas. I went back there six years ago. After driving about a hundred miles, I could swear it was the same telephone pole. Nothing, you know. After thirteen years in California, with the hills, and the beauty and everything, Texas, you know, goes on forever. And that's kind of what people do to their lives. That's why they are falling asleep all the time and driving off their road.

A new thought is like a rising road. You see, a rising road gets you higher and higher and higher, and you go up and up and up, and the higher you go the more you see, the more you're aware of, and the more you're able to understand it. A rising road leads us to see things in a clearer way, it leads us to see things in a better way, it leads us to see things in a larger way, because we're more aware of things happening around us. And we go higher and higher and higher.

When we get really high up on this road, we have to be awake because when you're on a high road sometimes there's a big drop. And what we don't want to be is like the person who was driving along and heard somebody yell, "Watch out for the cliff." And the response is, "What cliff?"—as they go over it.

The idea of you is you. And if you know you are the person you are looking for, the person you want to be, already, you are allowing yourself to flow with new thought constantly. "Today is my opportunity to be new, to be me in a new way." If that is your way and that is your affirmation, you will find something new about you every day. New visions will appear in every step along your way, and you will celebrate those new visions. You can let go and let yourself explore more of yourself, and something very beautiful happens to you as you do this. As you become more and more aware of the newness of you, the reality of you, the harmony, health, and beauty of you, you look around and suddenly find yourself accepting the same idea for everyone around you—every person, every place, every thing.

To be transformed by the renewing of your mind means to remain new in every moment. "I am new now, I don't care how new I was yesterday." If you are depending on your newness of yesterday, you are depending on something old, you are depending on stagnation. So we allow ourselves constant progress in our own understanding of self; constant progress becomes our normal state of being, and we flow in a harmonious, beautiful way. Constant progress at all levels of our life is nothing more than our sincere desire to be a better whoever-we-are, to improve whatever we are doing. All of a sudden we will see constant progress at every point along the way. And it's beautiful.

The idea, again, of you is you; and there's nothing that you are ever going to experience that is going to limit you. This is why many of us share the adage, and it's something that we have known in New Thought for years, that once you know this and apply this, you grow younger and younger and younger every day. To discover you is to discover the true meaning of you and the true joy of you.

Ask yourself these questions: "Is there any limit? Is there any end to progress? Is there any end to this power within us that leads us to a fuller expression of self and more and more accomplishment in a positive way in our continued progression in this thing called life?" No, there is no end to it. No, there is no limit to it. Therefore, there is no limit to you.

We never stand still. We CAN'T stand still. Many people try to stand still, and they just can't do it. That's why they keep running into things. They're trying to stand still. Trying to stand still is shoving yourself off the road. You see it all the time.

You can watch people trying to put the brakes on. You hear them talk, "Oh, remember the good old days? Remember when gas was a dollar? Remember how good it used to be?" My answer is "Well, that's good. Why don't you go ahead and dig the grave and hop in? Because you've ended it. All they have to do is throw the dirt in.''

The idea is to get yourself out of that. You are absolutely beautiful, and all the power within you is just waiting for you to let it happen as you. You never stand still. And when you know that and know you know it, you suddenly realize that you are forever ascending, higher and higher in understanding and higher and higher in experience of self. Greater life, greater beauty, greater happiness, NOW.

I continue in my treatment by saying, "As I let good fulfill itself as love, which is life, I let myself love the expression of myself. Because I love my neighbor, my work, my family, myself, I understand what love is."

And, people, this is a lesson I'm teaching in this Creative Thought Magazine: Unless you love your neighbor, your family, unless you love your work, unless you love everything that is happening as you, as yourself—and you can always get some idea of how people really feel about themselves by the way they talk and act and react toward others—unless you really let yourself love, unless you really let yourself be that, and unless you really let peace begin with you, you will not know what love is all about.

I go into this further. I say, "It is the infinite givingness of Divine Mind through and to Its creation. I am that creation. Therefore, I am love in action. You are that creation. Therefore, you are love in action. God loves the world by means of me.'' What a fantastic, magnificent affirmation that is.

People, if we could walk out of here today and affirm, "God loves the world by means of me," and let that be our way today, we would end the need for churches. We will evolve to the greatest thing that ever lived. One day on this planet we will give birth to the Christ-man—not the Christian, but the Christ-man—the illumined man, the person who has learned to function free from world concepts.

There is a beautiful book called, "The Gospel of Relativity," that talks about that, by Walter Starcke. I recommend it to you.

But this can happen as you *now*. If it is your goal but you do not do it all the time, don't put yourself down. We are all learning, we are all growing. We are who we are, and that's who we need to be. You are where you are, and that's where you need to be. And wherever you are, that's the only place you are ever going to start. That's the only place you are ever going to change anything. What you don't want to do is wind up over "here" creating what you had over "there." What you don't want to do is turn loose and do something over "here" and it turns out to be what you were doing over "there."

You are the only thing you are waiting on. You are the only thing your good is waiting on. You are the only thing your health is waiting on, your abundance is waiting on, your answers are waiting on.

Again, as we fill our mind, as we fill our heart with understanding, automatically we allow ourselves to fill ourselves with appreciation—self appreciation. "I appreciate what I know I am." Well, if you do, act like it! Say it! "I appreciate what I know I am." Do you? If you don't, do something about it. Because all it's waiting on is you. Once you learn to appreciate what you know you are, you will learn at that point how to appreciate everything else more and more.

And do you know what happens then? Everything starts appreciating you more. It has to be that way. There's nothing else it can do. We allow ourselves understanding, which evolves into appreciation, which evolves into love; and then we find ourselves flowing through life becoming more and more and more efficient in a positive way.

I'll tell you what I mean. This is a good way to explain

treatment; it's also a good way to explain what I'm talking about. Say we have three glasses of water here this morning. Water is water. It's one thing, isn't it? But say in one glass of water we take some tea and put it in. What does the water become? Tea. And this other water, we heat it up and put some instant coffee in it. What does that water become? Coffee. In the third glass of water we take a little dirt and throw it in. What does that water become? Dirty water, whatever. We have the water. Water doesn't care what we put in it, does it? But whatever we put in it, it becomes. And that's the same thing with mind. That's the same thing with the power within you. It is what it is. It is fluid. It has been described as ether, plastic, whatever. It is everything.

When you put something into it, that's what you have. Right? It is the same thing in your own life. Your thought is taking this clear fluid, whatever it is, and it is dumping it in there. And once your thought enters it, that's what it becomes as you. As the water becomes coffee, as the water becomes tea, as the water becomes dirty, it becomes what has been put into it.

Now, a lot of times what we are doing is this: we want, say, coffee; and instead of getting the clear water we get the water with the dirt. We put coffee in it and then complain because it doesn't taste right. And the thing in your own life, if you want to change it, you've got to dump the garbage out of it, get a clear start, and then put into it what you want. The water doesn't care what you put into it. But whatever you put in it, that's what it becomes.

And you can put a new label on it. "My water that's brown is now coffee." Well, God as you, Infinite Mind as you, Infinite Intelligence as you, is what you let it be through what you dump into it; and what you dump into it is what you are thinking about, what you have accepted as you. This is action. This is the action of mind. It, also, as

I said, helps to explain treatment. It must become you, as you, what you let it become, as you.

I continued my treatment by saying, "In this beautiful moment of limitless contemplation all that has limited my expression of self is now recreated in positive ways. I diligently apply intelligence and understanding to follow up my inner awareness in all that I do, say, and think."

And this is important, people. You must diligently apply intelligence to your life. "I diligently apply intelligence to my life."

People, it is less than intelligent to base how you feel on something that happened yesterday. If you want to heal it, you must empty your cup. You cannot have anything new unless you empty your cup, unless you get the things out that you don't want any more. The creative power of Infinite Mind is where? It's right here. It's right WHERE YOU ARE. Jesus said, 2,000 years ago, "You may search lo here or lo there for it, it is within you." Three or four hundred years later, they came along and established a church, and do you know what they said? They said, "It's up in the sky by and by when you die. You're unworthy, you must suffer, you must put dirt in your glass."

What you're searching FOR, you're searching WITH. If we let ourselves flow with this, we will understand very clearly that this power is everywhere at once, available to everyone; we can take as much of this power, people, as we believe in. You are never going to go beyond your level of belief, because if you did, you wouldn't know what it was that happened. You wouldn't even know it was there if it was there. We have to understand this. The Creative Power is there. But what are we doing? We're drawing on a storehouse, a storehouse of infinite good that is forever Itself. And no matter how much good we take out as our expression of life, there's always that much more left, and you are not taking anything away from anybody else.

Infinite Mind doesn't care how much good you accept today. The life you live is the level of your choice. So if we allow ourselves to know that, we suddenly become aware of, "I am in touch with AWAKENED thought"—not asleep thought—"I am awake to my now; and I know that as I am, the power within me is bringing forth in a positive way, because that's the way I choose; I refuse to live any other way; I dedicate myself to the best." Now, if I need a reason to do it, the only reason I need in order to have the best in my life is the right of consciousness, because that's what Mind will respond to.

Our understanding of the Science of Mind allows us to use this principle as ourselves. It allows us to make this manifestation possible. There's no limit to it. "A free mind," said one of the great teachers of the east, "is no more influenced by worldly frenzy than the moon is affected by earthly wind." This is the way we need to be. "I lift myself above and beyond this."

I had the opportunity twenty-four years ago to join the United States Navy and I spent four years in submarine service. It was a very interesting experience. I discovered something about myself. This was before I knew about treatment. Number one, I don't last too long on the surface of the water. One of the beautiful things about being on that submarine is that I rode out fifteen hurricanes in four years. A submarine can go down and the storm just goes right over it. You just sit down there and you're all just snug and warm. It's better than the storm. You can get out of the way of it. And it's the same thing in your own life.

We can spot storms, can't we? Storms of confusion, doubt, fear. Just get yourself out of it. If someone else is creating havoc in your world, let them just storm away. You don't have to be in it. If you're going to be in it, get a good raincoat and an umbrella, find some shelter. What is the shelter? It's within.

Again, a free mind is the awareness that you are the person you want to be, the awareness that you are the person you want to be right now. Being the person you want to be is nothing more than following through with self-transformation. It is allowing yourself to move forward at the level of intelligence where you are allowing the intelligent process within you to agree with something.

And listen to some good advice from the wisdom of the ages: "If you're going to agree with something, don't agree with anything but Truth." You know, many people think they have a truth, but it's not true. And if you believe you're limited, if you believe you are restricted, if you believe that you can't do something, that's a lie, people. If you're agreeing with that, that lie will become the truth. You'll say, "See? I proved it to myself. See how unhappy I am? See how miserable I am? See how this has happened to me?" That's a negative ego trip. You are drawing attention to yourself and you are drawing everybody else's attention to you—for a while. They'll all leave. If you want to be lonely, be negative. Even if you've got a lot of other people around —like attracts like—you'll have a bunch of other negative people around and you'll all share your loneliness with each other.

I conclude my treatment by saying this: "I joyfully realize that I am the person I have always wanted to be. I now move forward with this knowing. It becomes my wisdom. It celebrates my oneness with people, places, and things. The love, health, happiness, and joy of God, through me, is me, and I accept these in all my relationships." Not some. ALL. Every person, place and thing.

One of our students in class said a very interesting thing. You've all had this experience. At the turn of the year, from 1978 to 1979, all of a sudden you're writing out a check or something, and what do you put down? 1978. Okay? A secretary said in one of our classes that she was typing one day and typed up a whole series of letters and all of them had January on them, and it was February. Okay? What was typing the letter? What put 1978 when it was 1979? Do you know what does it? The mechanical mind. Your subjective mind is nothing but habit. And you'll have to remember that your subjective mind lives only in yesterday. That's why you must consciously awake to NOW.

The only way you can handle today, people, is with today's newness. If you're trying to handle it with yesterday's idea, you're in trouble. Today's newness is the only thing you can handle today with.

Someone told me about this program on educational television about a tribe of people some explorers found. They met these natives there and they gave this one native a twelve-inch ruler. They showed him how to use the ruler. And he was very excited. "Hey, look what I can do!" And he went around and measured his hand, seven inches long; and he measured the bowl he was eating from, and it was about eleven inches long; and he could measure everything else until he found things that were longer than twelve inches. And he didn't know how to handle that situation. So he found himself confused. He didn't know how to measure anything that was longer than his comprehension, anything that was beyond what he knew at that point. He reached the limit of his own comprehension as far as measurement goes.

The people there then gave him a yardstick. Now he had a whole new world to explore. He could go out and measure all kinds of things that he never could before. And he was really enjoying himself. But again, what he did was, he allowed himself to go beyond that limitation of one foot. The point, I think, in that, in my own observation, and the point I would like to make to you, is this: "Never believe

that the limit of your comprehension is the limit of life."
Do you hear what I'm saying? *"Never believe that the limit
of your comprehension is the limit of life."* Because all you
have to do is understand more of you; and then you expand
your comprehension and, therefore, you expand your application of self.

So flow with that, and know that there is a place within
you that is open to higher understanding. Why? Because it's
open to The Inifinite. Why? Because it IS The Infinite in
action as you. When the law of action and reaction works
through you, give it only what you want to experience.
Give the law of mind, through thought, only the things you
wish to experience in life.

What we are talking about is a mental action, not an
intellectual action. A MENTAL action. Intellectualizing
this concept is not going to heal anything. Sitting around
with a group of people and talking about this is not going
to heal anything or change your life. Sitting around and
making some kind of noise and thinking that you are medi-
tating is not going to change your life. The awareness you
have in action as you, as you move your experience, twenty-
four hours a day, THAT is what is going to change your life
for the better.

So let yourself realize the Divine nature of you, as you.
Fill your imagination full of the best, full of future possibility, as you. But know it is NOW. Know it is you right
now, and your evolution will happen in a beautiful way.

Infinite Mind manifests Itself through the individualization of your being—no one else's. You draw from the
Divine nature what? You draw your own unique expression;
and that's important, and that's special, and it's YOU. And
we should celebrate that. Allow yourself a conscious union
with the Great Whole, and as you do, you will know yourself as the Infinite Power in action in your world. This

power, this Infinite Power, you will know and know you know it is your only source, your only security. As you increase your awareness of that, you increase your efficiency as you, and you let yourself know, and KNOW you know that you are the person you want to be.

Let it be your way. Have a beautiful day.

The reader already knows that Reverend Jay Scott Neale is a native Texan, because of the humorous reference to it in his talk, "How To Be The Person You Want To Be."

Reverend Neale's professional background includes work in the theater, television, and radio. He was also a music critic for a syndicated news service.

His church in Fremont, California serves 3 cities in proximity to each other. In addition to the time he devotes to the ministry, which keeps him well occupied, Reverend Neale writes for Creative Thought Magazine. He also finds time for his radio program, "The Power for Good," and for his television program, "The Science of Mind," both of which are presented in the San Francisco Bay Area.

Reverend Neale gave his talk, "How To Be The Person You Want To Be," on June 3, 1979 at the Fremont, California Tri-City Church of Religious Science, which he founded 5 years ago.

CHAPTER SIXTEEN

For the law was given by Moses,
but grace and truth came by Jesus Christ.
                                            John 1:17

No Room at the Inn

Reverend Arleen Pitcock

Today's talk is titled, "No Room at the Inn," and I have had some conflicts about it from the standpoint of being more aware this Christmas season than I ever have before of the importance of accepting the real idea of Christmas. We need to put behind us the outer appearances. We need to set aside some of the things that are going on in the world, and in our own world: the conflicts, the emotions, the reactions. We need to come to ourselves, as the prodigal son did, to a place in our own consciousness of the awareness of what Christmas really means and what it is all about.

The Christian world is celebrating the birth of Jesus, and in Religious Science we are Christians in the true sense of the word. There are over two hundred Christian denominations in the world, so you might ask, "Well, what is Christianity?" But we clear it in our own thoughts, and we answer our own questions. The experience of Christmas should be a personal one. There are inner meanings to everything that is going on. There is an inner meaning to all of the reactions, to all of the experiences that we're having, to all of the conditions in which we find ourselves. There is always a symbolic thing behind them.

Somebody might say to you, "You look wonderful today." After that person leaves, you may say, "I wonder what he meant by that." There was a reaction within you that showed you took the compliment to mean something other than the words that were expressed. And that's what we want to get at. That's what we want to know and feel, so that we can live life the way Jesus lived it, which was to demonstrate the potential of the universe. We want to participate in it and enjoy its rewards.

Let's look at some facts related in the Book of Luke. There was a decree that everybody had to go and pay their taxes. The story is familiar to all of us, I'm sure, but I think it's important for us to just quickly review the situation so that we can see the "What does this have to do with me?" kind of thing.

Everyone had to go to his home city, and Joseph, who was of the house and lineage of David, had to go to Bethlehem to pay his taxes. He brought along Mary, his wife, who at the time was, as the Bible says, "great with child." She was ready to give birth while they were in Bethlehem. The birth was of Jesus of Nazareth. They wrapped him in swaddling clothes, and they laid him in a manger because there was no room at the inn.

All right, what does this mean? Why did the birth of Jesus have to take place in a manger in a stable and not in one of the inns of Bethlehem? According to the facts, there was great unrest and fear in the country at that time. There was the domination of King Herod. The majority of the people were not receptive to anything new of any kind. They were busy looking at what was wrong in the world. They were resenting and feeling helpless that there was nothing they could do about anything. They were experiencing personal unrest based upon reacting to the outer.

Symbolically speaking, "no room at the inn" means that one has a closed mind and that there is no place through which new ideas can enter. This is the house of self-satisfaction where we are so set in our ways that we will not accept any ideas which might disturb our household and cause discomfort.

Many times we put up a fence and a sign which says: "Don't bother me with the facts. My mind is made up. Don't throw anything at me that may cause me to have to rethink something that I'm believing in and that I'm living by."

Even though the results of that closed-mindedness may be uncomfortable, we are familiar with it, and we know what to expect. But when you are told, "If you give up your false idea and accept this true idea," you don't always know what is involved. Perhaps the things involved would bring out some of your fears. Maybe it will mean your having to make decisions you're afraid to make. Or that your world will change in a way you won't like. Or it might mean you will have to depend on yourself for something which you feel incapable of doing. Therefore, we become afraid and closed-minded. We respond with, "Well, I'd rather have this misery and know what to expect than open myself up to something different and *not* know what to expect."

Refusal to experience the discomfort of change deprives us of newness of life and of the natural unfoldment of creative ideas. People who look at the world of conditions, and who see that as all there is, have a right to be afraid; because if you look at those facts, there's no way you are going to get a sense of peace. There will be unrest and perhaps anxiety and disappointment. But again, we are talking about that which is behind those facts and that which created the facts.

People come into and go out of our lives continually for one reason or another. Perhaps there is a change of job, perhaps there is a move from one place to another. The first teacher I ever had said to me, when I was lamenting the idea of change and not being comfortable with it, "The only thing that you can ever depend on in this world is change, that your life is going to change. But that change does not have to be bad. That change doesn't have to be the same as changes you didn't like which you went through before. Change can be good."

If we believe that there is a power for good in the universe and that we can use it, we're not always willing to demonstrate that it is true. You see if it is true that we are a part of this power, "all that the Father hath is thine." Everything necessary for our richer living is available. But we don't experience it. We look at the tangibles. We still look to reason, rather than behind it, in order to discover what caused it in the first place.

All right, "no room at the inn" is the closed-mindedness. It's the filling of our consciousness with negatives of life: "I can't." "I can't do this." "I can't expect this person to change." "I can't because I'm too young." Whatever it may be, we keep on prefacing it with "I can't."

And the "Yes, but" is the same kind of thing. We say, "Yes, I believe God is good, but . . ." Then what? That means there's an exception. That means that God, the Principle of Life, made an exception to the rule. We frequently look every way around problems to find reasons for telling ourselves that in a particular instance it's not going to work: "In this particular instance I have found a problem which is more than God, or Mind, can handle."

And that is the house of self-satisfaction, the house of

false righteousness, when we believe we are smarter than that which created us. Because that is not true, we experience the results of the untrue belief. We experience struggle. We experience strain and pain. And we experience a sense of "fight"—trying to force something to happen.

The innkeepers were deeply immersed in the consciousness of the political situation; therefore, they did not recognize the opportunity to accept an idea of newness when Joseph and Mary knocked on the door. The inn was filled; in other words, there was no room for any other idea. They had given all the rooms to the angry people, to the resentful people. Those people didn't like paying their taxes, they didn't like being dominated. And that was the consciousness.

When our consciousness is filled with fear, anger, and resentment, our "mental household" is filled with those things. That's what we're open to. That is saying, "There's no room within me for anything else. There is no room within me to accept a new idea because I'm too busy being angry about the old stuff. I'm too busy being involved in my illness."

Many people say, "Cure me IN my illness," but they do not say, "OF my illness." They say, "Cure me IN my problem," but they do not say, "OF my problem." In other words: "Relieve me of the pain but for heaven's sake I don't want to have to change my mind, I don't want to have to get a new idea, I don't want to have to get rid of those old ideas of resentments and angers and negativity." Why? Because they are challenged. It is a threat which says, "I've lived life a certain way and I just don't want to have to change it."

It behooves us, I believe, at this time of year, to ask ourselves what kind of thoughts we have in our mental household. Today's news tells us about the annual trek to Bethlehem and that all the cars and all the people are being checked because there is a great fear of terrorists.

Christmas is a loving time but it can also bring out the worst in many people.

I was parked in a lot a few days before Christmas and saw a lady driving around looking for a parking place. I was going out. She drove up the aisle backwards. I said, "Yes, I am going out." I figured she'd go around and come back and take the place. Well, she didn't go around. She blocked herself and me. She was so fearful of losing that parking space that I couldn't even get out to give it to her.

Finally I got out of my car and walked over to her and said, "You realize, don't you, that your car has to move from there before I can go out to make the space for you?"

And she said, "Yes, that's right. You get out and then I'll get it."

And I said, "How are you going to park the car backwards?"

She answered, "I will. Don't worry. You just get out!"

So I backed out. She moved enough to let me out with about two inches to spare. I pulled way back to give her plenty of room. She pulled her car in, and she blocked the car next to where I was. She then turned the motor off and got out of the car and went off. All this with apparently no thought of what was going to happen when the people whose car she blocked came back. She was so filled with frustration that she apparently lost a good deal of her reason and logic.

All right, many people go crazy at Christmastime—not just in terms of what I just described. There is more plain depression than at any other time of the year. This is all based on experiencing Christmas in the outer: the gifts, the packages, the decorations, the food, the family, the relatives, the conflicts that each one of us might happen to be going through, and then having to get it all together. And it's magnified because so many people throughout the world are doing all this at the same time.

There are two extremes at this time of the year, generally: extreme highs and extreme lows. Both are artificially induced. Kids get high on the idea of the presents. The lows come from the people who have the feeling of lack. You hear things like: "I don't have the money for a Christmas tree, I don't have the money for the food, I don't have the friends to invite over." Or, "I've got all this and it hasn't made me happy, I don't know what's the matter with me, I've got more than I've ever had and I'm feeling miserable. Why don't I feel the true sense of Christmas?"

To the person who says, "I don't have money for a Christmas tree," I would say, "Neither did Mary and Joseph." I am sure they didn't have electric lights and whatever at that time. The point is there: outside pressures to conform. Man has created this thing to be as beautiful as it can be and has said that this is what you do and have to do in order to experience Christmas: "You have to have a tree, you have to have a traditional dinner, you have to have gifts, and the more expensive the better because that means you love me." I'm taking it to an extreme but follow along with it. Man says, "You have to have people around you that you love." Generally we've got people around us that we don't love and the ones we love are off with people they don't love.

So we've got all this set up; A, B, C, D, "This is what must be done to have a good Christmas." So everybody does it to the best of their ability and to the most their pocketbook allows. Then they sit back and wait to be happy. And then comes, "Where's this great love that I feel? I took my last five dollars that I should have used to pay the light bill and bought a present instead, but here's the gift and you darn well better like it." All kinds of things do we do out of a need for approval of others; but also it's a demonstration of our own sense of insecurity.

We can look at it this way instead: "It's all right that I

don't have the money for a Christmas tree this year. It's all right that I don't have the big fancy spread. It doesn't mean that I am poor in spirit. It simply means that I'm experiencing that condition in the outer right now.''

The freeing idea and the new idea is that one doesn't have to continue in the condition. Maybe this year it's not so good, but you can do something about your own consciousness and break out so that you don't have to accept the "poor" idea. Whatever the thoughts were that created the experience of "there isn't the money," something was done wrong in terms of thinking. Some ideas and some beliefs that aren't in harmony with the principle of life were accepted, that's all. Therefore, you can change them and have any kinds of experiences you want to have.

I said to somebody, "Do you have either a can of beans or a can of soup in the house?"

He said, "Yes."

I said, "Okay, put a candle on one of them and have a merry Christmas."

Why is the food so important? Here were Joseph and Mary knocking at all of the doors at all of the inns. They didn't go to the doors and say, "Now, wait, you've got to let us in because there's going to be the birth of a very important person, so let's *do* something here."

Okay, they knocked at the doors and there was no receptivity anywhere. But they didn't react; they knew the Truth. And when we know the Truth and when we know that we're all right and that we have something within ourselves to depend upon, there aren't closed doors. We simply don't belong there, that's all. And so they go to a smelly old stable. And when they looked at that, they did not turn up their noses and say, "Now, wait a minute, we can't have a Christmas experience in a smelly old stable, we deserve better than this."

Somebody called me up once and said he was looking for an apartment. He didn't have a dime in his pocket. He said, "I've been in Religious Science for fifteen years, and I'd like to have you do treatment so that I can have the right apartment."

I said, "Fine, I'll be happy to."

I did the treatment. He called me back the next day and he described the apartment he found. I guess it was cheap and it wasn't very clean or something.

I asked, "Do you have the money for it?"

He answered, "Yes, exactly."

Then I asked, "Are you going to take it?"

"Well, no," he said, "I'm above that sort of thing."

I said, "Oh, really? Do you have a place to sleep?"

"No," he replied.

I asked, "Do you have more money to pay for a better apartment?"

"No," he said.

I said, "Well, then what makes you think you're above that sort of thing?"

You see, we get very self-righteous when we learn that we can have perfection, that we can have everything we can conceive of as being good and right for us. But we forget that we cannot go beyond our own understanding, which is at the point of our awareness and belief. It says, "All right, here I am today. It's no big deal. Maybe I don't like where I am today, but I can do something about it."

And so Joseph and Mary gladly went into the stable. There was no resentment. There was nothing that said, "I can't do this, this is beneath us." They were grateful for a place. They knew that they certainly weren't going to stay there and that the Truth is always demonstrated. They had no inner reactions to what was going on in the outer.

They didn't have the anger and the resentment. They had a quiet knowing trust that the right people would be there for this birth, those who were receptive to it. They knew it would happen in the right place.

Now we come to the shepherds who were in the fields. They were away from the community thing, you know, the hustle and bustle that was going on, and away from the dominating idea of being under the influence of a ruler—which is simply the ruling idea. They were watching over their flocks of sheep—which means they were in control of conditions, because the sheep represent thoughts, metaphysically, and they follow. Our thoughts follow and manifest our experience. As shepherds we are shepherding our thoughts. We are refusing to think of anything except, "This is what I choose to accept in terms of Truth."

Since they were in the fields and away from all of this that was going on, they were able to be objective and they were receptive to the news from an angel. Angels represent spiritual ideas. An angel is a divine idea that has been revealed.

And since they were in an area of quiet, they were receptive to the inner revelation of Truth that a Savior was born, and this brings great joy to all people. A Savior represents a saving idea. Giving birth within each one of us to the Christ-consciousness brings great joy to all people because that Christ-consciousness is available to us at any time we want to experience it, at any time we open up the doors of our minds, our thoughts, and allow that Christ-self to be made known in our experience.

This is the season of spiritual communication. It should be. But what are we communicating? Is the dominant idea the decorating and all the other outer things?

The Book of Matthew tells of the wise men who followed the star which led them to the stable. Wise men represent spiritual resources that bring form through spiritual revelation. Spiritual resources mean within—within consciousness. The three wise men represent the trinity of man—spirit and mind and body. The star represents intuition—being open and receptive for divine spiritual ideas to reveal to us whatever it is that we need to know. In treatment, we say, "Divine Mind reveals to me that which I need to know when I need to know it." That's what they were doing. They were receptive to it. Wise simply means wisdom. Joseph represents wisdom and Mary represents the spiritualization of love. So when you have wisdom and love coming together in a consciousness of wholeness, you're giving birth within yourself to the Christ idea.

The gifts that the wise men brought were gold, which means riches of the spirit; and frankincense is the beauty of the spirit; and myrrh represents the eternity of the spirit. Well, what is that except consciousness of wholeness? Those are spiritual resources that we all have within ourselves and which are always available.

Why was Jesus born in a stable? The symbology behind that is that there is a sense of openness. It is open to wise men, which means spiritually aware. Animals, to me, represent the idea that God is everywhere present. There are no high or low levels of consciousness. There are degrees of awareness that are available. And that stable was available to anyone who was receptive—to those that intuitively knew that something had happened. The shepherds came down from the hills to partake of this because they knew that something important was taking place. It is an idea that is available to everyone, not just to a chosen few.

When we are receptive and open to saying, "The Christ idea is within me and I choose to give birth to that idea today here and now,'' that's fine. We have all been exposed to the ideas of eternal life, to wholeness, to perfect health, wealth, Divine love. But Jesus was an individual who held the universe to its claim. And he devoted his whole being to the manifestation of these old ideas. He opened his mind and his heart to life and received in return experiences that bore witness to his trust.

Jesus the Christ. The Christ means the God idea in the absolute in man that man has personalized. The name Jesus represents the spiritual idea of man. And The Christ represents that God idea in expression.

And so he took the idea. He lived it. He proved it. He believed in it. He trusted it. And that's The Christ idea. We are thankful for that example. But it's up to us, in order to experience Christmas, to choose to move forward into our own expression of divinity. We can only show as much of God as we can reveal in our own life. Each Christmas is one more opportunity to see this.

In Genesis, God said, "Let there be light." That means wisdom. All right, at Christmastime we should all say to ourselves, "Let there be light. Let there be that light based upon wisdom and love within us that means let it be brought forth within my consciousness."

Let each of us bring the Christmas light to fruition, but not just at Christmas. That's just a reminder to us. We have every day of every year in every way an opportunity for each of us to demonstrate it. We can say that our consciousness is open and receptive, that there is room for newness, that there is room for the expression of love and creativity, and that there is room for the rightness that prevails everywhere in life. But that rightness is according to an immutable law of mind. And when we tune ourselves into that law we can make changes that are absolutely fantastic.

No Christmas tree. So what? The sin, or the failure, in my opinion, is when we don't recognize the Christ idea within ourselves. When that is recognized, we can do something with it. And what we can do with it is free ourselves, express, and expect and experience a greater sense of love and joy.

Reverend Arleen Pitcock has been a minister of Religious Science since 1975. She served as assistant minister of the churches at Fort Lauderdale, Florida and Monterey, California prior to her assuming the pastorship of the El Cajon, California church in July 1979.

She is a native Californian, having been born and raised in San Jose. Prior to her commitment to the Religious Science ministry, she spent 19 years in the business world as an executive secretary and business administrator.

She received all her training through Religious Science International, beginning her studies in the Napa Valley Church of Religious Science in 1964.

The talk, "No Room at the Inn," was delivered by Reverend Arleen Pitcock at the Fort Lauderdale church on December 24, 1978.

CHAPTER SEVENTEEN

I am not to blame for my life,
But I am responsible for what I do with it.
—Taliaferro

Life's Perfection

Reverend William M. Taliaferro

This morning I would like to free associate with you about whatever comes out, whatever the feeling is. I had an interesting meditation this morning, and I think some rather profound treatment, in order to allow myself to become open and be a channel of free-flowing wisdom and intelligence. And I feel free. I am going to share whatever it is that needs to be shared that is coming from the depths of wherever it may be within me.

Each person in this room has a challenge in living life. Each person within a New Thought teaching, a metaphysical approach to life, has a challenge that perhaps the majority of the people in the world are not even aware exists. There are a multiplicity of things within that challenge, but I think we can bring them down to some common denominators.

The first challenge is to find out who you are. That sounds very simple. Find out who you are. If you find out who you are, you're going to have to, by virtue of the nature of the way we are taught to think in this type of thinking, throw away some of the games and patterns you've been holding on to. That's going to be the first by-product of finding out who you are.

The second by-product of finding out who you are is the necessity to take a point in time to live it—who you are—and to live it without concern about who anybody else thinks you are, but to stand for who and what you are, and live it, and let the chips fall where they may. And if other people don't like it, tough. That's their problem, not yours. It becomes your problem only when you allow it to become your problem; and at the moment you would allow it to become your problem, you would no longer be operating on the construct of having discovered who you are. You would again be trying to live up to who somebody else thinks you are.

There are some interesting techniques that go beyond the personality to find out who you are—the who you are that goes beyond the physical being, the who you are that by its very nature proclaims to you, "I Am That I Am."

"I Am That I Am" is probably one of the most difficult statements in the Bible to really understand. But it's essential that we understand its impact because *there* is where we begin to establish what our identity is, who we truly are.

When we say, "I Am That I Am," what we are actually saying is that whatever there is in the universe that is creative, that is the life force, that is the spark of intelligence and wisdom, that is the essence of life itself, I am *that* "I Am."

Jesus says, "Before Abraham was I Am." "Before anything was," we could add in paraphrase, "I Am." "I Am" meaning "the completeness of the life force; the totality of the life force I Am." There's absolutely nothing missing. There is no part of that I Am-ness that we embody that is not totally and fully complete at the moment of conception, and before and after.

We have the necessity to function within the framework of a body on this plane of existence. Yet we are limited by the body. We have a very definitive need to communicate with words and with semantics. However, we are limited by the semantics that we use because we tend to identify ourselves as the body, first of all. Second, we tend to identify our thoughts with our words. And that's just as limiting.

Let's think a moment about the whole business of semantics. The moment I say, "God," you have a construct of thought that is uniquely yours. You may share it with somebody else, but the chances are that your own construct of Deity is completely different, or slightly different, from somebody else's. So when you say "God" to me, I haven't got the faintest idea what you're talking about—absolutely none. I am still in my own life and awareness developing for me a construct of Deity that I can understand, that is not limited. And since my construct changes from day to day and, hopefully, becomes larger, what I said yesterday is God in my life may not be what I say today is God in my life.

Those of you who have been in classes with me for some length of time have said, "Well, two weeks ago you said this, and now you're saying that, and that's different from this." And my response is, "Yes, but two weeks ago I was not the person that I am today, because what I am today is changing and evolving and expressing in a different place from where I was two weeks ago. Otherwise I'm not growing."

If I am my body, I am finite. If I am my word, I am finite and I am limited. And the Bible tells us clearly, "Know ye not that ye are gods?" and ". . . these things that I do ye shall do greater." Those two statements are sufficient to indicate to me that I am not my body, that the body is the vehicle through which I express. And I'm not my words, because my words are simply my method of attempting to communicate my thoughts.

Most of our thoughts are not terribly clear. Therefore, our words are not terribly clear. Yet we identify with our thoughts and our words. Most of us when doing spiritual mind treatment attempt to operate on the basis of being definitive, and much of the time we are not definitive. And we lay on mind a treatment that by its very nature is not explicit, and we expect to get explicit results. And we don't. We scarcely realize that mind cannot respond with specificity to a demand if the input was not specific.

We are continually impressing upon universal subjectivity, upon the universal unconscious mind, our concept of who and what we are. And Mind then says to us, "Whatever it is that you choose to be and wish to be, you are,"—that is all, you are—"and I will see to it that you become that."

We are continually impressing upon Universal Mind the concept of our thoughts with the words that we use. Then Mind says, reasoning, that whatever we're saying is correct; and it gives it to us. Since we are Intelligence, there ought to be some kind of message in there—whatever it is that we think of ourselves, Mind, God, being infinite, says, "Yes, you are." Then we become that. And then we deny that we did it, we deny that we had any responsibility for becoming that which we perceive ourselves to be. We blame our parents; we blame our teacher; we blame our minister; and we blame anybody that we can put in a position of authority. And yet it is exactly that concept which produces in our lives what we are.

I don't think we ever reach the point of finding the totality of who we are. However, when we first get that glimpse and that awareness and that wholeness of who we are, I would like to think that we could never be the same again in terms of the way we think. I would like to think that once we recognize that we are playing a game with life—and whenever we play a game there's a winner and a loser—we had better make sure that the game that we play makes us the winner and not the loser. That means that we must accept the total responsibility for who and what we are.

Well, who are you? I Am That I Am.

Let's use the moment of conception as a starting point. I am not sure that scientifically or spiritually it's correct, but let us assume for the moment that it's correct. At the moment of conception there was an absolute perfection within you. There was an atomic intelligence—if you want to use that term—that told every cell how to divide, how to build muscle, how to build tissue, how to develop bone marrow, how to develop nerves, how to develop the organs, how to develop the senses, and so forth. And we didn't have to tell it what to do. It knew. There was a wholeness and a completeness, an atomic intelligence functioning in there.

Somewhere along the line—let's assume it happened at birth or shortly after when we first got hungry and didn't get fed—a sense of "but I'm not perfect because if I am perfect my needs would have been met" started developing. This is not conscious choice that we made. It is the result of an experience that we chose. The nurse or the mother is late bringing the bottle so I am uncomfortable, I am hungry, I am wet, I am this, I am that. And that means that I am not okay. And we start laying a matrix of thought and feelings and experiences across this perfection that knows how to do everything that needs to be done within our bodies.

If you wanted to look at your life at this time in terms of experiences, you could look at it in terms of, let's say, sixteen layers of Kodachrome film. Kodachrome film consists of three pieces of film superimposed upon each other with a gelatin filter in between. The gelatin is a different color. When you put that film into the developer the gelatin dissolves and the three layers are melded together, and that produces what you have. If it's perfect exposure you get a perfect picture. But you know what your pictures look like when you underexpose them or overexpose them. That's what we do with our thought. That's what we do when we layer these matrices of experiences and race memories upon this perfection. The perfection that normally has a free channel to go through life, and to express, becomes twisted and filtered so that by the time it comes out at the top in life it's not the same as it was, or was intended to be, on the bottom. The true identity down here, that I Am-ness that each of us is, is now warped. It's discolored. But it is the same I Am. It never changed in the perfection that it was in the beginning. We changed it.

So what do we do? Well, we start to really find out who we are by peeling away these matrices of memory and experience that we've laid upon ourselves—to get back down to see that I Am-ness, that wholeness, and that completeness, and that perfection. And do you know how to do it? You do it by daily meditation; and you do it by spiritual mind treatment; and you do it by making a demand upon mind to reveal the truth of you to you as you. It sounds complex but it's very simple.

You can sit down quietly sometime today and say to yourself, "I want to know who I am, I want God to reveal it to me in a way that I can understand. Father, reveal yourself to me in a way that I can understand." Having made that demand upon Mind, become receptive and listen. Be receptive for a feeling. Expect a glimpse of insight.

Feel a wholeness starting to permeate your being. Hear a constructive thought that gives you the feeling of having dominion over your life. Once you get these, hold on to them and make a further demand. The neat part about Mind is that, being infinite, you can make demand after demand after demand, and you can do it as quickly as you choose, and as quickly as it responds to your demand it's ready to respond to a new demand. There's no limit to how many demands you can make. But once you get this glimpse of wholeness and completeness, once you get this glimpse of okay-ness, once you get this glimpse of absolute atomic perfection operating in your being, you begin to understand the truth of the statement, "I Am That I Am." You begin to understand that you are not you but that you are the vehicle through which the I Am-ness expresses; that you are not your words, since your words change because your thoughts change. You begin to find that your vocabulary becomes more concise. You find that things which come from you are different from what they were before. Even if the words are the same, there is a feeling that has changed. There is a gentleness and a tenderness, an exposing of raw edges.

It's okay to be vulnerable at that point. It's okay to express that I Am-ness because no one can ever take it away from you; no one can ever hurt it; no one can ever clobber it; no one can ever insult you; no one can ever limit you; no one can ever do anything to you any more, because you know that the I Am-ness within you is perfect and complete and dynamic and that you are centered in that I Am-ness, that wholeness. Then other people's opinions are truly none of your business—not from a defensive point of view; not from a point of view that says, "Go mind your own business;" but from the point of view of being able to sit back and dispassionately say, "Well, gee,

I understand where you're coming from but I don't share that at all, I don't feel that way about me.'' There is no power in that. But the moment we vest with power what someone else says about us, or relates to us, we're back again laying on those matrices of thought that are going to limit us and put us right back in the box.

It's a challenge to find out who you are. It's a complex challenge because there is a part of you that really doesn't want to know. I mean, if you're honest with yourself, there's a part of you that really doesn't want to know. Each one of us has played many games over the years. Most of those games are limiting and self-deprecating. Most of those games are self-limiting devices to prevent us from expressing wholeness. There is great comfort in familiarity, especially pain, especially lack of joy, especially lack of spontaneity—because it means we're different from the rest of the people if we have those things. We don't want to let go of those games. So, if you really think about it, you'll admit it. You would like *to want* to get rid of the games, but you really don't want to get rid of them. It's like stopping smoking. I have said, ''I would like *to want* to stop smoking.'' But I don't want to stop smoking. And until I want to stop smoking I'll never quit smoking. So I don't worry about it any more. I would like to want to be able to stop smoking, but since I don't really want to, mind responds and says, ''Well, you're not going to.'' Well, then, I won't until I decide that I want to. Okay, that's a game.

The game of feeling inadequate is a beautiful game. It's called P. L. O. M., poor little old me. We develop this desire to have the world feel sorry for us. We play this game of ''poor little old me, the world just did me in, no one understands me. My boss won't give me a raise. My wife doesn't cook for me or clean the house the way I want her to. I don't have enough money. I can't go on vacation." And on and on. That's a game. We don't want to give it up because it's comfortable. We know the limitations of the game. We play it very well and there's no reason to give it up—because if we give it up we will have to replace it with something else. There would be a void. If you strip away this defense mechanism, what are you going to replace it with? Mind, operating as it does, says, "No, you don't want to get rid of that game." And it does everything it can to hold on to it.

We talked some months ago about the law of subconscious finalism—that the subconscious mind will win, it will win even in conflict with the conscious mind. Tell your conscious mind anything you want to tell it. It doesn't make a particle of difference. The subconscious mind wins the battle. So the work has to be done at the subconscious level through meditation and treatment.

What happens when you rid yourself of a self-limiting device? All of the energy that has gone to maintain that device, to maintain that game, to maintain that structure, can now be used in a constructive manner instead of in a destructive manner. You begin to express more energy, you begin to feel more vibrant about life, you begin to feel whole and complete about yourself, because you are gradually releasing the games. And then you say, "Bye bye, I don't need you any more. You served a beautiful purpose. You got me to survive all this time, but now I see you for what you are—a lie, a perversion of me, a perversion of the truth, a perversion of the force that is perfect within me; and I don't need it any more." And one by one we go through them and we get rid of the games.

Perhaps we never get rid of every one of them. But at least we will have something to work on for the rest of our lives. At least we will have a starting point from which to express that "I Am-ness." At least we can start allowing that perfection that knows how to do what needs to be done, to express.

And that's a lot better than walking around saying, "All's well with the world," when your world is not well at all. To me, that's the ultimate hypocrisy. "All's well with the world"—but your world is going to hell in a handbag, your health has gone down the tubes, your finances have gone down the tubes, your relationships have gone down the tubes, and you just scream these affirmations into the void, "God is good, God is great." But add to that, "not in my life." Otherwise, stop using the affirmation, because every time you make that statement, the subconscious mind is saying, "Oh no you're not! Oh no it won't! And you know it, and I know it."

How do you feel when you stand in front of the mirror and say, "Be still and know I am God"? How do you feel when I or anyone else stands up here and says "You are perfect, spiritual, and divine"? How do you feel? You and most people don't feel terribly comfortable with that awareness; because that means that you're in charge. That means you're in control. That means you have absolutely no excuses any longer for what it is that you're doing to yourself. We don't do anything to anybody else. We can't. But we sure do it to ourselves.

When you know who you are, when you know that "I Am That I Am," you start accepting the responsibility for your life, totally. We grow up. And that's what this teaching is all about. We grow up, we stop blaming people, we stop wasting energy on people, and we bring it back "here," where it belongs.

If you're really busy on yourself, you haven't got time to worry about anybody else. You're too busy within, working and expressing more of that I Am-ness. And that's who you are.

I hope I've given you some ideas this morning of how to find the I Am-ness in your own life, how to expose it in your own life, how to allow it to come out in your own life.

If I have said anything, I have said that you started out perfect, you are perfect right now, even though you may not appear to be; and you will always be perfect. Therefore, why not act like it? Why not reconstruct your identity? Why not bring yourself back to the starting point, which is wholeness, completeness, an atomic perfection? Why not allow yourself the privilege of being who and what you are? It's where you started from, and I can't see any reason why we shouldn't go back there at the beginning. Change the past. Change your idea and concept today.

Start revealing.

Reverend William M. Taliaferro has been a minister in Religious Science since 1976 and was the pastor of the Church of Religious Science at Eugene, Oregon until February 1980. At that time he assumed the pastorship of the Church of Religious Science at Fort Lauderdale, Florida.

While at the Eugene church, Reverend Taliaferro was the Northwest Regional Director for RSI as well as the District President of the International New Thought Alliance. He is currently serving on the Board of Education of RSI.

Reverend Taliaferro had his ministerial training with Dr. Earl Barnum at the Church of Religious Science at West Valley, California.

The talk, "Life's Perfection," was delivered by Reverend Taliaferro at the Eugene, Oregon church on September 24, 1978.

CHAPTER EIGHTEEN

Don't always do something,
Take time to sit and dream,
And let your dreams be big.

—Whitehead

Take Time To Dream

Dr. Carleton Whitehead

Many years ago the prophet Joel wrote that young men dream dreams of what can be, and that old men dream dreams of what might have been, and that it is the type of dream they dream that keeps them young or old.

I would like to share with you a story of a dream come true, a dream that kept a man young. I want to tell you how and why it came true and what transformed an ephemeral dream into a dynamic vision. In this story are the ingredients which you and I can use, to make our dreams come true. To paraphrase Shakespeare, "Dreams are the stuff that life is made of."

A number of years ago, I was driving along the north coast of Jamaica looking for a place to spend a few days. Five miles or so from Montego Bay, I saw a beautiful pink stone wall with an archway, and a small sign that read, "Holiday House. Guests. Accommodations." Intrigued, I parked the car and walked through the archway into a bit of paradise: tall, stately palms, beautiful shrubbery, lovely flowers, marvelous swimming pool, and six guest apartments. The graceful architecture was unique, creatively using the native pink stone.

A lady in the garden greeted me. "Yes, we do have an apartment available." We ascended an open stair to the second floor and a breathtaking view of the beautiful blue Caribbean framed in coconut palms. The charm and peace of the place permeated the very walls. It was the answer to prayer—but not just mine, as you will soon see.

During the week I talked to the owner, Mr. Stetson. When I congratulated him on what he was building, I was puzzled by his response: "Oh, I'm not building this." I had seen him out there directing the workmen, no sign of an engineer or a foreman or of anyone else supervising the work. Later I asked him what he meant by his statement that he wasn't building the new structure.

He answered, "Oh, yes, I'm directing the pouring of the concrete and the laying of the stone and that sort of thing, but I am not building it. *The dream* is building it."

He was too busy for conversation so I inquired no further then, but I was tremendously intrigued. Here was a man, probably in his seventies, who looked about fifty. He was obviously young in body, mind, and spirit; and filled to the brim with enthusiasm. At the first opportunity after our initial conversation, I asked him to tell me what he meant by his comment that "the dream" was doing the new building.

This was his story: "About ten years ago I came down to Jamaica with a large power-plant construction company that I worked for at the time. I really fell in love with this part of the island and I thought that it would be a wonderful place for my wife and me to have a little place. And that was all really that there was to it—at the time."

He related that when the power-plant in Jamaica was finished he went back to Boston. Every once in a while when there was a severe winter, or a hassle of traffic, the dream of a place on the shore of the Caribbean came back, and each time, it took on a little more substance. It is important to note here that there is a vast difference between the kind of dream from which life is made—and mere wishful thinking. Perhaps a better term would be "wistful thinking." "I would like this, but it is just not possible. It would be fine, but it is too much to ask for."

Mr. Stetson did not indulge in wistful thinking, nor did he clutch at the idea. He simply let the dream grow in substance in his consciousness.

About five years after the dream began, Mr. Stetson asked his son, who was going to Jamaica, to look for some vacant land along the north shore. His son found a beautiful piece of oceanfront property about 300 feet long and 250 feet deep. Mr. Stetson's response, when the son phoned him about it, was, "Get an option on it." And then the sale went through.

A year later, when Mr. Stetson retired, he and his wife began to build on the property they had acquired.

Mr. Stetson told me that the dream—at least the portion he saw of the dream—was for just a home, plus a guest cottage for friends who might like to come down from the north on occasion. He said that the dream continued to grow and that he "just followed it."

After the house was underway and they were living in part of it, the dream said to him, "Build some guest cottages because there are going to be other people who would love to be in this place."

Thus the idea of this two-story six-unit guest home began. Mr. Stetson had no architectural training, although he did have some engineering experience. Therefore, his first thought was to hire an architect. Then he decided to just wait and see what the dream would do.

Step by step the dream unfolded. The whole design of the place came forth, including the design of the swimming pool. And I've never seen another swimming pool like it. It's beautiful and large, but not with a pump and a filtration plant. Fed by the ocean, it's like a tidal pool. The ocean currents continually flow through it, keeping it clean. It's absolutely lovely. All through the place there are these little ingenious elements. It truly is a paradise.

And the dream continued to unfold. At the end of each season, Mr. Stetson would look at what the profits were, and the profits dictated new construction for the following year. He never borrowed a dime for the whole thing. The dream supplied everything that was needed.

You see, he didn't reach out to grasp the dream and try to hurry it. And this is the first element in a dream becoming the experience. The first thing to do is let a dream be what it will, because a dream is a Divine idea emerging into your awareness from the Divine Mind within you.

Mr. Stetson's desire to live on that beautiful coast is what gave rise to the dream. And so the unfolding of the dream is letting it be. Oh, he cooperated, of course. You could see his cooperation all the way through. And he worked—only he didn't call it work. Everything he did was a joy. He let the dream unfold, and he had a complete willingness to follow it. This is the meaning of the words, "Thy will is mine."

What a completely different idea this is from saying, "Well, I will bend my will before the will of God." Almost always, when you hear people say that, the "will of God" means to them something less than what they truly desire. It means a shrinking rather than an expanding of the dream.

But how could there be any Truth in that, with a God

of light and love? How could there be any Truth in that, with a Mind that is infinitely greater than we can comprehend?

The will of the Infinite One must be far larger than what we can conceive. So when we say, "Thy will is mine," we are letting our will blend with the larger one and we are doing what Mr. Stetson did. He let the desire and the first little dream—a small cottage and a guest house—expand. I could see the building of the new units and the final idea. It was a twenty-unit complex, and it was all done gracefully and magnificently and it looked like a dreamhouse all of the way through. Truly a bit of paradise.

He LET this unfold. He was willing to follow. He was saying to the dream, "Thy will is mine."

At one point I mentioned to him the term, "Religious Science," and when I saw it met with no comprehension I let it go. But I knew that no matter what you call what he had, it was the Truth. Well, he didn't call it anything. It was something that he did intuitively because of his attunement with life.

So, regardless of what label you put on the creative action of mind and spirit and the marvelous law through which it flows, it is the one power that flows into a dream with all of the substance necessary to bring it into outer manifestation.

The second point is to not push. Mr. Stetson didn't get all excited because nothing happened in those first five years. He *let* the dream lead the way, simply taking one step at a time. With joy he watched the dream come into manifestation. He didn't hurry and he didn't pull back. He just followed the unfoldment.

When he mentioned the third point, I would have sworn

he had read my book, "Can You Keep A Secret?" He said, "I didn't talk to anyone about this. I didn't even talk to my wife about it at first. I knew she would love the place. I just kept it to myself. But really I didn't keep it to myself because I didn't try to hold on to it. The dream kept returning; and each time it did, it became stronger. The first time I mentioned this to anyone was when I heard that my son was going to Jamaica. At that time I talked to my wife about it and said, 'Honey, what would you think of getting a piece of property down on the north shore of Jamaica?' She said, 'Wonderful.'"

Oftentimes we get an idea, a dream, and we say to a friend, "Don't you think this is a great idea?" The friend may be polite and say, "Oh, yes, that's fine." Or the friend may not be so polite and, thinking he's doing you a favor, will say, "That's ridiculous! It won't work." What happens to the dream? If it isn't dissipated, it's at least tarnished.

Keep your dream between you and the spirit of God at the center of your being. It will speak for itself in due time.

As I walked through that archway, the dream was speaking loudly and clearly. Mr. Stetson didn't have to tell me about it.

Keep your dream to yourself. It's not necessary to ask the barber or the beauty operator for advice. If you need professional assistance from an architect or an engineer or a financier, get that assistance. If you need assistance in following your dream in a spiritual way, see a practitioner. But keep the core of the dream to yourself until it gets so strong that it naturally unfolds in the wonderful way that it did for Mr. Stetson.

William Carruth touches a common chord in his lines:

"We are all of us dreamers of dreams;
   On visions our childhood is fed;
And the heart of a child is unhaunted, it seems,
   By the ghosts of dreams that are dead."

What happened to these young dreams we have all had?
Did some "wise" elder discourage them? Did you hear,
"Don't sit there dreaming—*do* something"? This can be a
crushing blow to the rich, God-given imagination of a
child. How truly wise elders would be to say instead:
"Don't always be doing. Take time to dream and let your
dreams be big!"

Ten years ago I had the privilege of seeing a "workshop" belonging to a lad of fourteen. There were pictures
of trains and locomotives of all types and vintages. Book-
shelves were lined with histories and lore of railroading.
Models were everywhere. Bud's dream was to be a railroad
engineer. If adults had learned that this was anything more
than a hobby, they probably would have pointed out that
railroads were on the decline, jobs would be scarce, there
were greater opportunities elsewhere and therefore this was
a pretty foolish dream. Fortunately, Bud kept his dream to
himself except for two or three people he knew he could
trust to let him dream. I just heard the thrilling news that
Bud, at twenty-four, is the youngest engineer on one of the
country's major railroads.

How sad when youngsters take the word of their elders
who want them to be out doing and let their dreams die.
Carruth closes his poem:

"'Tis a cup of wormwood and gall
   When the doom of a great dream is said,
And the best of a man is under a pall
   When the best of his dreams is dead."
"He may live on by compact and plan
   When the fine bloom of living is shed,

But God pity the little that's left of a man
   When the last of his dreams is dead.''
''Let him show a brave face if he can,
   Let him woo fame or fortune instead,
Yet there's not much to do but bury a man
   When the last of his dreams is dead.''

We are very fortunate that we are glimpsing the fact that dreams do not have to die. In fact, it is the dream of what can *be* that keeps us young. So, no matter how small or how great your dream may be, dare to dream it. Dare to affirm that with God all things are possible—no matter what the human opinions may be. Dare to let your dream gain strength in your consciousness, to come alive in your imagination. And then let the very power of the Creative Spirit move it before you into manifestation, with you following along and doing your part joyously. Remember age has nothing to do with it. Titian had the dream of painting a masterpiece when he was in his nineties. He painted it at ninety-nine.

Never take to heart that old bromide: ''I'm too old to dream.'' That's like saying God in you is too old to dream.

If your dream of what you can be has weakened, resurrect it. It may or may not be a dream of success in the world's eyes. It is what it means to *you* that counts. If your dream is of what you can be and do as a person or what you can be as a spiritual light in your life and world, dare to dream it. Dare to know the substance and power in a dream. And dare to follow it to the glory that it holds for you.

Dr. Carleton Whitehead delivered his talk, ''Take Time to Dream,'' in 1979 at the First Church of Religious Science, Chicago, Illinois, where he has been pastor for the past 10 years.

Previous to his affiliation with the Chicago church, Dr. Whitehead was pastor of the Church of Religious Science at Monterey, California for 17 years. He took his training with Dr. Harvey S. Hardman at the Mental Science Institute, Denver, Colorado and was ordained in 1950.

Dr. Whitehead's previous professional background is that of a civil engineer.

Offices he has held with Religious Science International are: president (1962 to 1966), and chairman of the Board of Education (1971 to 1976). He is currently the district president of the International New Thought Alliance, Illinois-Wisconsin.

Dr. Whitehead is well known for his writings as well as for his ministry. His works include: "Creative Meditation" (Dodd Mead 1975), "Can You Keep A Secret?" "This is Your Life," and "Mind and Medicine."